I0214344

LIVING ALIGNED

BY KATHRINE MITCHELL

Copyrighted Material

Living Aligned
©2020 by Aligning Inc.

All rights reserved. The text of this publication, or any part thereof, may not be reproduced in any manner whatsoever without written permission from the author. Some names and identifying details have been changed to protect the privacy of individuals.

Library of Congress Control Number 2020916279
ISBN: 978-1-7321658-1-6
Printed in the United States of America

Cover design: Steven Gagliano

DEDICATION

*For Miakoda...the light that always
shines brightly to bring me home*

TABLE OF CONTENTS

TABLE OF CONTENTS

INTRODUCTION
INTEGRITY

REALIZATION
TRUTH
UNITY
CERTAINTY

REALIZATION

I believe we are in unity; one interlocking link with a Universal Consciousness.

I am this energy every moment, every day, of every year I breathe. We all are. My intuition tells me this Universal Consciousness is similar to what we feel on this Earth plane as unconditional love.

After years of practicing as an intuitive and interacting with family, friends and colleagues, I have gathered that we are all searching for this one thing called Love. Not any old love we share with a boyfriend, parent or even child. What I attempt to define is without restriction; it has no words to express itself.

I have felt its power, and it has prevailed for me time and time again. It is Magnificent and Magical. It has the ability to cross all threads in time and space. It cannot be bought, found or even denied. Unfathomable. It can heal with mere thought and from it emerges the meaning of Trust.

As far back as I can remember, I felt a physical separation from this unconditional state. I think at one point, we all have.

I was challenged by my family's traditions and what society hoped for me. I struggled with feeling inhibited in a world where all I wanted was to be liberated. Their ideal relationships, politics and religion—even God being a male who lived beyond my reach—possessed so many requirements that felt impossible to fulfill.

All of it simply did not resonate with me as an everlasting unlimited support system.

I had no choice but to discover the true meaning of faith; however influenced I felt, I had to put my trust into someone else's words and actions over my own. I was torn by a conflict between my head and heart, and still I continued to search. I knew I would not settle for anything less than a path that would help me comprehend the meaning of unconditional love.

I remember it was a weekday morning. I was watching the sunrise sitting near the ocean on Fire Island when it occurred to me that the dysfunction in my life and all of my questioning had forced me to choose something different.

It was then when I made the decision to stop searching. I did my best to detach from the limited perception of what I knew and what I was told to be or do. This did not happen overnight—but the timing was just right. I discovered that what I felt was displaced so long ago. A newfound feeling of peace and a sense of courage would be at the foundation of every step I would take from that point on. In the search for unconditional love, I had discovered my integrity.

TRUTH

We are unconditional love; a blissful state that resembles an earthbound love we hope to find one day. I do know the attempt to find it would lead to an endless journey, as it is impossible to find something outside ourselves that already resides within us.

We will need to find patience on our quest to rediscover what integrity truly means to us.

We must be ready to make a decision with the hope that an opportunity will present itself; a possible option for us to return to our natural state of living without provision. This journey of exploration will begin here and enable us to embrace all of life's experiences—the happiness and heartbreak—and lead us to know what works for us and what feels right. Ultimately, we will come to know our truth.

UNITY

Integrity is not only to be true or honest. It is a sense of peace. It's holding ourselves accountable. When in integrity, there is no questioning our identity because we are certain of who we are: a wholeness residing within our being.

Unity. We express compassion not only for ourselves, but for all whom cross our path.

Oneness. We do not identify what is right or wrong; however, we act out of the "Right-Action" and not a "Wrong-Action." Or, simply put, what actions we believe within ourselves to be the right course versus a misguided one.

The origin of the word integrity is compared to integer: something complete on its own, like a whole number that is not a fraction. Consider this: when a number is split, it is still whole. For example: when the number 1 is split, it becomes a 0.5 and a 0.5. The split is evident, yet each division can become whole again. We know this because our education has taught us the conflict or separation happening is temporary; we are fully aware the 0.5 came from the 1, which is the original source. A whole, single source.

CERTAINTY

When we experience challenges, we may feel disconnected from our Higher Intelligence (also known as our Higher-Self). This conflict replaces the feeling of oneness with uncertainty, doubt and fear.

This struggle is real, and perhaps it may help us shift. It is possibly pushing us to look at ourselves in a new way. Although it will require a bit of work, we must hold on to our integrity and be patient. When you remember you are aligned and supported, living divided from the whole is not an option. We are complete, even when we feel disconnected or separated from our unity.

When we recall that we are still connected to our original source and who we truly are, we will no longer just make it through the events of our lives, but rather focus on creating a life filled with Love and Infinite Possibilities.

In my world, there is no such thing as coincidence. I believe this book is in your hands because it is where it needs to be. It has found you so that you may prepare for this modern spiritual movement.

INTRODUCTION

I know we are on the verge of a powerful discovery. I am also aware we have some time before our world moves forward, merging the gap between science and spirit. Even though it may take decades or a few centuries, we should not concern ourselves with this because you and I have chosen a path of transformation and inspiration. It is possible you have been bestowed the responsibility to set a living example to inspire others, so at one point many more will have a clear understanding of our link to the Higher-Self and the Omnipresence.

I feel it is possible for all living beings to experience Bliss, a place where suffering is optional. The words written and examples offered to the reader is a starting place. The breath with The Eight Second Rule and the tools available to help us remain in our center can be your beginning. If you are committed to *Living Aligned*, you will progress in your practice with awareness, with patience to live from the Heart Center and with guidance from your Higher-Self.

Trusting in our Higher Intelligence becomes our natural state once more, recognizing the oneness of our unconditional love and peace.

PART I

FOUNDATION

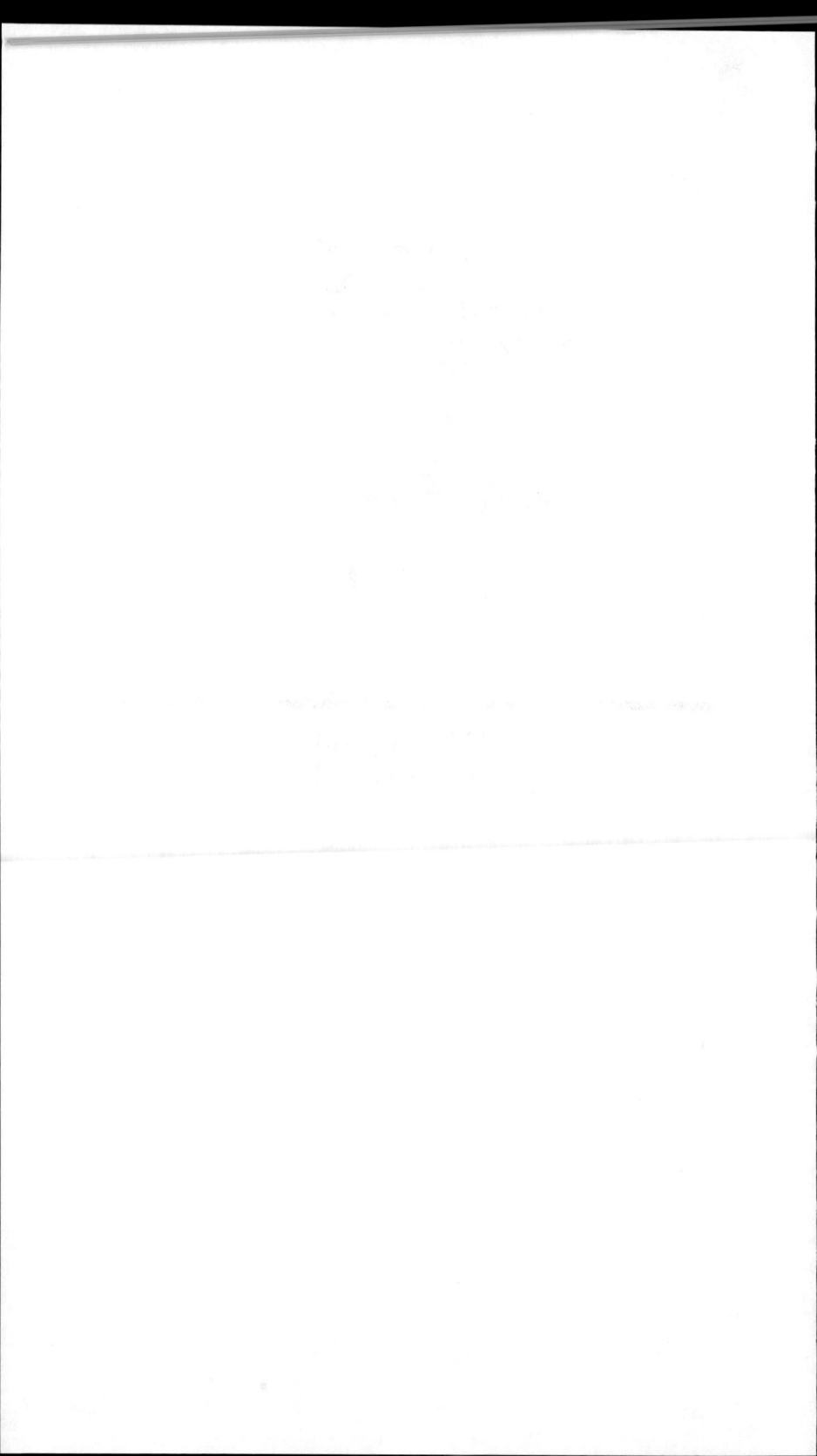

CHAPTER ONE

BEGINNING

INSIGHT
PRACTICE
HOME
RETURN
ALLIANCE
BELIEVER
COMMITMENT

Truly there is no beginning, as there is no end. We are aligned with an immeasurable energy that defines our limited view of time. However, I need to start somewhere, and this is where my Aligning story begins.

INSIGHT

I recall walking down the narrow hallway with my second grade class, making my way to the school library. Soft spoken, I asked the librarian for a book on my birth sign, Virgo. This small book sat perfectly in the center of my palms as I read, *"You will be an amazing nurse, teacher or someone in service to the community."* I sighed and thought, *that's it.* I shut the book with a feeling of disappointment.

Arriving home that afternoon, I pleaded with my mom to branch out to the public library. Happily, she agreed. I had a master plan to discover more on this fascinating topic of astrology.

I was intrigued with the subject of planets moving throughout our solar system, and in some way, aligning with my life events. The planets Mercury and Venus seemed to be important; however, at the mere age of seven, these topics were not easily comprehended. Nonetheless, they opened the door to what would become my life's work and pilgrimage.

Crossing the threshold of adolescence, I began to have a stronger intuitive insight; an internal voice which sounded much more confident than I felt. It supported me throughout my days of being bullied and abused, allowing me to feel some type of assurance—possibly even safe at times. What had truly occurred was the beginning of a deep-rooted trust within myself.

This act of trusting had appeared odd, as it defied the "normal" stages of growing up and figuring things out. I made difficult choices to develop a state of surrender, acting on Right-Action: what felt right for me; not what I was told could be the right thing to do.

This was not an easy task. It left me feeling like I had a great responsibility. Most of my relationships, including friendships, did not always understand me. There were so many moments in my life I felt burdened, and consequently at times, isolated. Although it felt challenging, I knew somewhere deep within my heart I had made the best possible choices for my life. I could sleep at night and stand up for what I believed in with no guilt or regret.

My conclusion was this: I had discovered my Higher-Self.

Reminiscing on this experience, I realize I've always believed there was something beyond this earthbound realm: an Omnipresence, a God or Higher Consciousness; it did not matter what I named it. What was important was knowing I was interlocked with this grand energy.

Most times in my life, I felt I was being supported—almost carried—through many of my turbulent times. I say "most times" because I do recall doubting this support when things were not going the way I wanted.

But even in the disruption of what I saw fit for myself, I knew I was still taken care of.

PRACTICE

I began to explore all possible paths to understand the complex connection to the Higher-Self. Several years had passed as I focused on strengthening my intuitive practice. I recognize now this was when my shift began. Personally and professionally, I began researching meditation and crystals, as they were the first to resonate with me.

College classes would be the next step, as I dove into the psychological mind of human behavior. I recaptured my passion for painting, as well as read everything on religion and spirituality. I discovered Feng Shui, an ancient art of placement; Reiki, a method of hands-on healing; and the Chakra System, which was founded on the sacred philosophies of Hinduism and Yoga.

A teacher training of Hatha Yoga inspired a commitment to practice The Eight Limbs Path—referring to the aspects of the yogic path—which provided me with the tools to create the Intuitive Yoga workshops.

All of these actions empowered my calling. In addition to all of my studies, I had stumbled upon a little book called *The Tao Te Ching* (pronounced: *The Dao De Jing*). It was founded on Zen philosophy. The 81 verses inspired by Lao Tzu would help confirm my profound belief that we are aligned with a higher source.

HOME

I like an adventure: traveling to discover new things about me, our world and the people that claim the big cities and small towns as home. I've visited a handful of high energy places on the East Coast that I feel connected to: Fire Island, Montauk Point and the Catskill Mountains, with so many more on my list to explore.

In the Arizona desert, there is one place, a sacred space just about two hours north of Phoenix; a little town named Sedona. The Red Rocks are miles high; the skies are crystal clear and a vortex of energy is elevated out there in the Southwest.

Sedona had become a yearly destination since my first wondrous journey there. Amazing events unfolded for the decade during my numerous travels that transformed the rest of my life. One such extraordinary experience occurred on one of my earlier travels in 2002 while hiking Sedona's Cathedral Rock.

I heard an external voice.

What I mean by external is that I could hear a voice ring somewhere inside my head; however, it was not my own. I know it sounds strange, odd and even amazing at the same time. (Please keep in mind my intuitive practice at a young age was founded on what I felt, heard and saw, and was not always defined or supported by rational means).

The voice was pleasantly faint, much lighter than my own, yet powerful and resonated as a female vibration. I heard a gentle demand with minimal or no emotion: "Go home, because you are a Home," with the mention of returning in nine years.

I would not understand the full statement until years later.

I felt confused. The message was not clear, and I was frustrated with the thought of cutting my travels short. Add an unfamiliar voice demanding I return home, and that was enough to leave me unsettled. Of course, I did as expected: I debated, then I resisted. With a bit of hesitation, I decided to remain for what was left of my four-week stay.

While meditating and hiking daily surrounded by red rocks, the external voice grew louder and more stern to return home. I should have expected several events to follow to shorten my stay in Sedona. Unfortunately, all these signs ultimately pushed me back to the East Coast ASAP. As the plane landed, I finally acknowledged this was where I was meant to be; a feeling of comfort came over me.

Days later, I discovered I *was* truly "home." I was pregnant with my beautiful, compassionate girl, and she was born the following January. She has taught me so much about integrity, unconditional love and the strength of an emotional bond. She showed me what home really means.

That journey helped me to accept that all experiences have some form of purpose. Some life events may be clear about offering us insight or guidance, whether we like it or not. At times, we will understand the purpose, and at other times, we cannot.

RETURN

In the years following my daughter's birth, my priorities were to be the most amazing mom, manage life as a business owner and be the best wife in a marriage that was struggling. During this time, my intuitive internal dialogue had weakened. It became a mere muttering of undefined words. Even so, my aim was to remain focused and be patient, as I attempted to be guided by my Higher-Self. Soon after my marriage ended—taking with it my so-called identity—my life had collapsed like an old brick building.

I was extremely sad and overwhelmed as I tried lifting the burden brick by brick off of my heart. What kept moving me forward was the knowing that I still felt connected, even though I had never been further away from my spiritual practice. I knew my Higher-Self was right there waiting for me to remember.

It was a late spring morning. The sunlight was streaming through the open blinds. I opened all the windows on the first floor, creating warmth as the sun filled the space. I think it was the first day in a long time I decided to rolled out my yoga mat.

After an intense emotional practice while resting in Savasana, I realized something I had forgotten: the universe has always provided for me. With that thought, I decided to make a request. I asked to rediscover my connection to the Higher-Self.

Only days had passed when my friend Amanda and I discussed a summer trip to Sedona. I felt hopeful, inspired and looked forward to our journey to one of my favorite destinations.

I felt optimistic about my decision to head out West; however, lingering in the back of my mind, I had an immense amount of personal and professional chatter. I was at a crossroads in my life, wondering where my journey would take me. My practice had always been a focus, and I felt confident guiding clients as an intuitive. I knew I was ready to expand to what was meant to be next; however, I had concerns about how I could contribute to the children of our world and help others who felt lost to regain their connection. Business was in the midst of change, but that couldn't be my only focus. I had to look at the bigger picture: I was also in a state of transition in my personal life.

I felt the shift happening again, and a need to surrender to the transformation. Most importantly, I had to trust the process on how this would factor into the next part of professional journey; it was not something that I could force myself to just figure out or understand quite yet.

Reminiscing about this time in my life, I believe I was on an unconscious mission. I had an intention: I was going to speak to the universe. I would ask the question: "What is it that I need to do?"

ALLIANCE

"You Have All You Need."

Landing once again at the Phoenix airport, Amanda and I tried to contain our excitement. We drove approximately 120 miles in 100-plus degrees surrounded by the intense emptiness of the desert. The sun was setting on the dry land and its oddly shaped cacti. As the day became night, the sky transformed into divine colors of pink, orange and lavender.

Finally, we arrived at our hotel, where we impatiently dropped off our luggage and headed out to Cathedral Rock. It was a short drive under a moonless sky to reach this massive rock located in the Coconino National Forest in Sedona, where the summit elevation is approximately 4,900 feet.

I was not surprised to find the perfect spot waiting for us. We parked.

In all my years visiting Sedona, I've hiked and practiced yoga many times during the daylight hours, but I had never experienced the environment this way. I was immersed in the dark, as there was nothing between me and this enormous red rock, except the scent of summer and the sound of stillness.

I could feel a subtle energy vibrating all around me, which made me look up with the expectation that I would see something—and I did. I was enamored with the night sky; it was breathtaking, with at least a billion stars dancing upon the red rocks that summoned me to their sacred space.

Amanda and I chatted for a bit, sharing how wonderful it was to be back in the desert. We fell into a comfortable silence, enjoying the quiet, and I felt as though I was meditating, as a dreamlike feeling of being centered had come over me.

Although the moment was serene, the question still stirred at the center of my mind: "What do I need to do?"

I was fueled by a dire need to have an answer. Privately I asked, "Universe, I need your guidance. What do I need to do?"

I sat still for some time, until the silence was ready to be broken. Startled and surprised, I heard a female voice. She said, "You have all you need."

The voice sounded familiar. I was sure it was similar to the voice from nine years ago—the one that had urged me to return home.

The voice echoed, "You have all you need."

The statement was repeated: "You have all you need."

Amanda spoke softly, with a bit of excitement in her voice: "Did you hear that? Someone just told me: 'I have all I need.'"

You cannot imagine the rush of adrenaline I felt. A confirmation that someone was listening and providing an answer.

For approximately one and a half hours, information was shared—information that I believe was to be extremely valuable for the world at large. What happened would alter the rest of my life. The guidance I requested suddenly appeared, with a nudge towards the next possible step of my journey.

Here is a brief overview of what was shared:

"An unconditional state gives you the ability to create with a foundation of unlimited potential. To create unconditionally is your right. It has been so since the beginning of time. On the physical plane, it appears you are limited to do so. You can only see it as a tangible energy, where something eventually will deteriorate or will end. What is unimaginable is not unattainable; it is something you have yet to bring into physical form.

"The steps to access Infinite Possibilities would be to work with the energy of no expectation and non-attachment. It is necessary to provide compassion and non-judgment for one another as you live as an alliance. This state of being unconditional is what you know as *Love* on the earthbound realm. *UNCONDITIONAL* would be the only word I, as an ethereal energy, could express to you to define this state of wholeness.

"On the earthbound realm, you link to the Illuminated Self, which consists of Bliss, Love and Surrender. When you recall this ability, you will design an experience representing your authentic Self. This fact lives within you; however, the loud voice of the mind overrides the infinite intelligence of the Higher-Self. When the lower-self and Higher-Self once again prepare to merge, a possible shift will occur. The shift will be unique to all individuals, yet will be unified based on all living creatures as they are aligned as one vibration. When ready to heed the call, create the tools that will assist you. The gifts of your home have it buried deep within its core."

I was then shown a symbol (), crystals of pink and clear quartz and the metals of sterling silver, copper, gold and titanium. Before the experience had come to its end, I heard this final statement:

"An unconditional state will be required, so that you may access complete communication to the source. Here is where you will begin to comprehend the direct link to that which lives within you. It will become a choice to rediscover your capacity; the ability to utilize your intuition to create and be in peace."

BELIEVER

The Blue Apple.

I am a firm believer that we are linked to an all-encompassing loving energy. I suppose these beliefs have helped me to have trust in my ability as an intuitive and perhaps in life, too. However, I had never been keen on channeling an energy, or would ever claim I could hear the voice of a goddess, angel or guide; honestly, I'm not sure I ever made a conscious choice to.

That evening at Cathedral Rock, my thoughts took over as my mind linked into this so-called reality of living on a linear line. I call it the "Live Line": a line where only our rational mind makes decisions; miracles and intuition do not apply. All we believe in is the line we walk, living a limited perspective as to what we see and what we have been told.

Only a few minutes had passed, but they were very long and difficult, as I became tangled in the Live Line state. I was struggling with the message I heard, wanting to believe it so desperately. I wanted to surrender to it, but it all seemed so unreal.

I believe the burden and sorrow I carried played a part in my doubt. I thought about the way our children are being treated throughout the world; it made the statement "You have all you need" appear as an impossibility. I felt, and still do feel, the innocent state of a child needs to be protected and completely provided for. And yet, some of our children are dealing with the tragedies of homelessness, hunger and abuse in our world.

In that moment, I wondered, how could we have all we need if these acts of cruelty and betrayal are still allowed? I apologize if this has disturbed you in any way; that is not my intention. It is my own endeavor to one day help conquer these issues and create a safe, healing space for our children.

But these thoughts created a battle between my mind and heart. I was quite skeptical: if I have all I need, well then I can ask for anything and even make demands. I could feel the rush of adrenaline once more. As I write this, I know now what was shared that night could not be comprehended with the Live Line's small mind, but still, I needed proof.

It was here that I made an unusual and impossible request.

I spoke out loud.

My voice trembled with a nervous energy.

I slowly lifted my right hand, palm facing up and fingers open and ready to receive.

I requested a Blue Apple.

I grew impatient as a condescending smile began to form.

Intensely watching the outline of my right palm...

No. Blue. Apple.

Well, the night was still magical, even if I didn't receive what I asked for. Although there was no blue apple in my hands in that moment, I still had the stars and an enormous red rock to be grateful for.

The next morning, I was still trying to digest the events of the night before. Amanda and I agreed to step away from trying to understand anything more, deciding we would lighten things up and attend a friend's barbecue in West Sedona. We stopped by a local organic grocery in the center of town to pick up veggie burgers, buns and fruit for a salad. I was craving nectarines and decided to add them to our list. Amanda was helping me pick out the ripest ones.

I couldn't stop my thoughts from wandering to the events on Cathedral when I heard someone calling my name. "Kat, Kath… KATHRINE!" It was Amanda, requesting I look down.

Before me, in clear view on my lower right side, near the weaved brown basket holding at least one hundred nectarines, were the words "BLU APPLES" written in red on a bright sunny-yellow colored package.

A thunderbolt of energy, almost like lightning, shot through my entire body. My jaw dropped and my body trembled; luckily, my feet were planted firmly on the ground. I must have looked like one of the Warner Brothers' cartoon characters, as my eyes opened wide with astonishment.

It was here. Right here. The "Blue Apple" I had requested.

The two blue apples came in a package: one for me and one for my friend. These plastic apples are meant to keep fruits and vegetables preserved for weeks longer in the refrigerator.

Today, my blue apple sits on my night stand on the right side of my bed. I awake each morning with the knowledge that I am completely provided for. I think back now, smiling and wondering, what would I have done if it were an edible Blue Apple?

COMMITMENT

The experiences which unfolded over a course of fifteen years bring me here as I write the last few sentences of the first chapter. The need to share my discovery has been one of the most important commitments I have made since being out West. I experienced a connection out on the red rocks that summer. It was rooted with the intention to once again align with my Higher-Self; to reconnect to unconditional love.

Having this link to unconditional love fostered my understanding that we have all that we need within us. We need of no thing.

Upon my arrival home, you can imagine the state of Bliss I felt. I had truly returned home. What I thought was impossible... appeared. The symbolic Blue Apple provided me with proof, which I no longer needed. A miracle happened. Or perhaps, it was simply the reminder to anticipate Infinite Possibilities.

The appearance of the Blue Apple poetically aligns with my whole story, as well as my life's purpose. It is the Aligning Method at work.

This illusion of separation from the Universal Consciousness and the Higher-Self will lead to a never-ending search to fill the void and is a waste of vital life energy.

We must remember it is our natural born right to feel, express and be Love. This state is the closest to what we know as being unconditional, and when accessed, we will experience our journey without judgment, uncertainty and fear.

Hidden within my stories, I've attempted to infuse the method of *Living Aligned*. Imagine a bridge built precisely between two places for you: where you are now, and where you would like to be. It is my wish that the words written will inspire this next stage for you and offer simple steps to once again *Live Aligned* with your Higher-Self.

PART II
CONSCIOUSNESS

CHAPTER TWO

MINDFULNESS

SURRENDER
ABSOLUTE
HIGHER—SELF
BREATH

SURRENDER

A red ribbon rested at the top of the entrance above the front door; white candles were well placed for good energy; and my siblings and I had rosary beads dangling somewhere near our beds. A tribe of people entrenched in many superstitions (a.k.a. mom, dad and extended family) raised me with a foundation that there was an all-mighty energy to watch over me.

My mom was more expressive of her religious beliefs as a devout Catholic, sharing her stories of the rituals of Christmas, Easter and the day of the saints. As a child, we would randomly step into a church and light candles in bright red glass holders for our loved ones in need and for people I knew I would never have the opportunity to meet.

I recall it was late July before my 16th birthday. I was thrilled as we embarked on our first-ever travels to a foreign land. My family—aunts, uncles, cousins and the whole clan—drove up to Saint Lawrence River in Quebec, Canada, where the Shrine of Sainte Anne de Beaupré resides.

The clear blue sky was a backdrop for the brilliantly designed structure and grounds that carried the scent of fresh cut flowers. It has been said by many that miracles of curing the sick and disabled had happened there. I suppose it was one of the reasons we traveled that almost nine-hour journey.

I have a vivid memory of one particular evening. We were attending a ceremony at the church, the highlight of which was an amazing walk along the grounds. We were given a small cup, and at its center it held a slender white candle lit with a tiny dancing flame. Walking quietly with my father by my side, among family and the crowd of hundreds of people, only the light of our candles illuminated our way through the darkness. The experience affected me intensely, and I began my attempt to understand this meaning of faith.

Surrendering to the little light that shined onto our path so brightly, we were able to safely take one step at a time. There, my thoughts silently expressed a great revelation: what I held was a link of faith and trust. This light resides within us.

By the end of that summer, I discovered what it was to be mindful and made a conscious decision to explore the foundations of other spiritual practices. I expanded my own belief system beyond an organized religion, and can now understand why it would take over several years to experience my own epiphany.

The process of faith would be converted to trust. This discovery would lead to my liberation and a bridge to enlightenment.

ABSOLUTE

Most spiritually-driven practices have many names for an all-encompassing energy: God, Jehovah, Odin, Great Spirit, Omnipresence, the Universal Consciousness. I personally do not think it matters what I call it because I am confident we are all linked to the same energy. I believe this consciousness is an energy that lives within us. It has created all things in the likeness of itself, not as an appearance, but as an infinite force of vast, limitless energy. It comprehends and understands the threads, the shifts and the evolution of what is sacred. It is absolute. It is something much larger than all of us and cannot be grasped with a simple state of mind.

This grand energy is aligned with the Higher-Self; our Higher Intelligence, essence or soul. It also reflects our lower-self, where we live in human form on the Live Line—or the earthbound realm.

It's important to remember when we define either the Higher-Self or lower-self, it should not be seen as a positive or a negative, but rather an equal function with a different purpose.

HIGHER-SELF

The Higher-Self and the Universal Consciousness have their own unique language. The communication is interlocked with unconditional love, an expression defined only as a vibration or a frequency. The communication exchanged is not something the mind can comprehend because it is beyond the mind's understanding.

We cannot translate this vibration with the mere spoken word; it is not limited to one's worldly language. It would be like stepping outside in below-zero-degree weather; the cold is a feeling, not a word. This comprehension is experienced on an unconscious level and felt where the heart resides in the body, at the Heart Center. It is where we are guided and intuitively trust our Self. In the Aligning Method, we call it the Internal Compass.

To simplify: I believe Universal Consciousness and the Higher-Self have a direct communication. Instead of words, the Higher-Self sends a frequency we feel at the Heart Center. The heart then interprets this vibration, and our mind transforms the message into thoughts, words or something that is relatable.

Let's explore how we as humans on the Live Line can connect and become a part of this sacred communication.

BREATH

Take a breath.

Inhale and exhale.

Breathe deeply and observe the expansion of the lungs.

You can feel how it is one of the most incredible things the body does, along with the heart beating and the extreme complexity of the brain. I bet this is why the great yogis relate to the breath as our vital life force. When we breathe, the vital life force keeps each and every one of us living here, and therefore linked to the Higher-Self.

A few years back, I created a series of classes called Intuitive Yoga. The foundation for the program is breath and movement, and the intention is to assist the student in becoming properly aligned physically while connecting to their Higher-Self.

Exploring the powerful yogic method intensified and deepened my own practice. The experience opened up my mind to what the sacred act of breathing is, which many of us take for granted in our daily life.

It's obvious the breath keeps us alive in the human form. It also brings our focus into the present moment, helps us gain self-control and reminds us we are safe.

Breath will have us check in with what we're doing, awaken an awareness of our actions and bring us home into our body. It supports our body, brain, intuition and the creative process of life. It is a magnificent energy flowing through us.

We have the ability to feel this power if we stop and observe nature, when we are swept away by the harmony of our favorite song or touched by someone we love. Breath is connecting us to this Universal Energy.

I would like to share a thought about this powerful energy that is our vital life force:

"You were created as a magnificent machine designed as an all-encompassing experience. Within it holds an intelligence of physical, emotional, mental and spiritual mastery necessary for all components to perform in its state of excellence. The structure must be clear, balanced and secure, so the electric current or energy will flow through all pieces, properly utilizing the interlocked system it was made to be. If aligned properly, the lower movement and higher movement will perform in its optimal state.

"If this mechanism is not connected to its source of power, it will lay there and appear lifeless; therefore, not accomplishing its service to the community or to oneself."

Imagine this electric current is the breath.

Are you breathing fully and deeply, so oxygen can reach all levels of the brain and body? If not, you may begin to feel sad, tired, unclear or disconnected, as well as stressed and anxious.

Unfortunately, a disconnect has occurred in the human form at this point. The body is no longer aware of its optimal health and spiritual intelligence. If a doubt that we are connected to something powerful has materialized, we will feel a detachment from the vital life force. Then, the limitations of the mind will dominate our mental and emotional responses and we begin to make decisions on autopilot.

I'm not sure if we are conscious of how we choose to breathe, but our breath must be complete; a full inhale and exhale. This will allow the brain and body to have balance and receive the full capacity of our life force.

Therefore, the breath is the foundation for *Living Aligned*.

CHAPTER THREE

LIVE LINE

WITNESS
LINE
STORY
INDISTINGUISHABLE

WITNESS

This morning, both my mind and all my senses were awakened before the sound of the alarm. I was wondering how I could truly describe the Live Line. I debated between turning on my laptop to do a bit of writing or heading to the beach for a bit of yoga first. My bedroom window showed me a crystal clear sky. I'd been writing intensely for days, and it felt right to take a break for some care-taking. Happily, yoga won out over my computer.

I've observed that a shift occurs in my consciousness whenever I'm driving the eight or so miles over the Robert Moses Causeway to the beach. I think I look forward to it as much as being near the ocean itself. I parked as close as I could to the boardwalk. I stepped out and sank just a bit as the warm sand welcomed me, a feeling of calm and balance starting to set in. I could hear the waves of the ocean. Then I felt a few drops of summer rain, which quickly became a full blown rain shower.

Intense. Every step had its own life. In that moment, time stood still and appeared transparent.

The rain made me homebound earlier than I imagined; however, I felt an inspiration as strong as the ocean waves. It felt amazing to be present and to recognize my choice to appreciate the rain rather than be disappointed to forgo yoga that morning.

I was fully aware and witness to the present moment.

I think having an awareness of our everyday interactions is a good place to begin our life's adventure. Unfortunately, most people are busy thinking about things that are truly not relevant in the present moment. Like, right now: where are your thoughts? I would hope on the words you're reading, and not on what you need to do tomorrow.

LINE

Every single living creature has an experience on the Live Line. Life unfolds into a mental, emotional and physical journey in the human body upon the earthbound realm.

As demonstrated in *Image 3.1* below, the beginning of the line is where our life in the human body begins. Where the line ceases to exist, so does the human experience. We all have a beginning, and we will also have an end.

It is only here on the Live Line where we will question our mortality, as well as our immortality.

What was before birth, and what will happen when the body dies?

I think philosophers and sages have asked these questions for centuries—and it's a conversation for another time. It's simply important for now to understand the finite nature of the Live Line and the infinite beyond it.

Image 3.1

BEGINNING ———————————————— END

LIVE LINE

STORY

I'm a big fan of the mighty movie screen, from supernatural, romance and fantasy, to the real life recollection of people and inspiring experiences. The few hours spent with the characters on the screen take us away; it's almost as though we are written into the script.

Our senses are alive as we experience the relationships unfolding, empathizing with each character's feelings of joy and triumph or sadness and tragedy. The emotions become a part of us.

When we leave the theater, the pretend place we just visited doesn't really exist, and fortunately, we realize this. We leave the story behind and make our way home.

Our thoughts and feelings are created very much like this. The Live Line is like a movie. Living on the line is like a picture show of our own stories unfolding. Our mind has created a story written, edited and filmed by us. Our memories become a trailer for the big screen of life and we will access them for all the days of our lives.

It tells our story, where we have a past, a present and a future.

On the Live Line, we are somewhere in the middle. Where you see yourself on this line is not dependent on your age, wealth or beliefs. You, me and the person you were sitting next to earlier today are at the same place.

Here. Now. Present.

We are in this very moment. *Image 3.2* on the following page reflects this concept.

Image 3.2

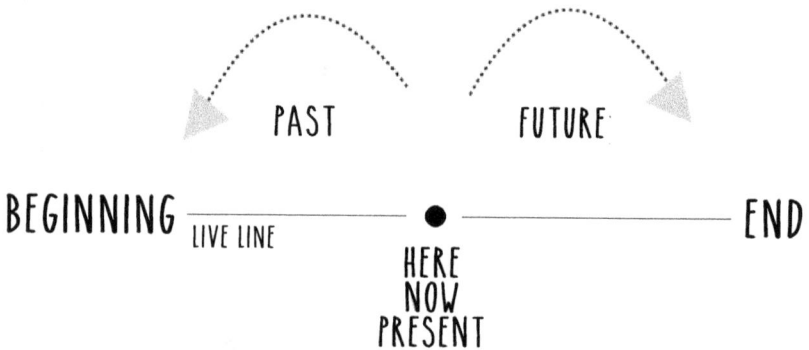

PAST   FUTURE

BEGINNING ——— LIVE LINE ——— ● ——————— END

HERE
NOW
PRESENT

In the present moment, from where you stand, you can see your past and say, look at what happened. This is my past. Looking forward, you see your potential outcome, and think, this can be my future.

From this perspective, I see a fragmented state of being; a sliced up space limited by a view of how you see yourself and the events that have shaped your life. A partial timeline keeps you contained within the limited capacity of your mind, where we see things in sections and break down life events so we may comprehend and prepare for our next life experience.

Then. Now. When.

We must use this strategy to understand reality because our mind is not comfortable within the unpredictable world. Actual life events are truly unknown to us and are constantly changing. If we choose to be in the now, our attention will be focused on what is here before us and we would have no room to be distracted from what is in front of us.

The present.

Awareness of our present moment on the Live Line allows the past, as well as the future, to fade away.

INDISTINGUISHABLE

The Higher-Self resides above and beyond the Live Line. It is aligned with our clear life path. It has a capacity called Infinite Perception, which means it is able to see, feel and hear an abundant amount of information linked to the lower-self.

We experience an indistinguishable space that is linked to what is beyond our comprehension. It is a possible journey we cannot recall within our mind, like developing in the womb, living a past life or perhaps spending time in another dimension.

We can attempt to understand this concept and fail, as our thoughts can only acknowledge what our memory allows. This is demonstrated in *Image 3.3* on the following page.

Image 3.3

HIGHER –SELF : SENSING WITH INFINITE PERCEPTION

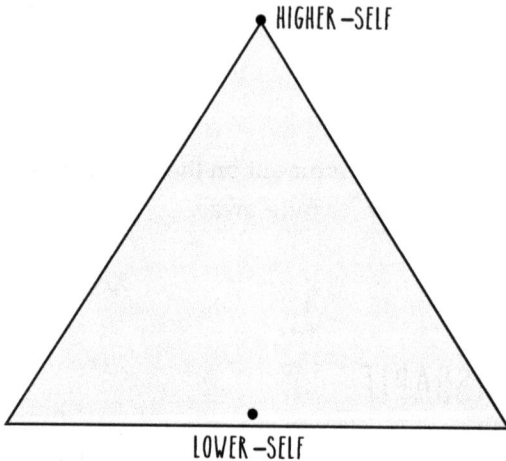

HIGHER –SELF

LOWER –SELF

LIVE LINE : LOWER –SELF : LINEAR VIEW

Now that we have a cognitive understanding of the conflict of living in the past or future, we can adjust our perspective to become more present, letting the now lead us to alignment.

CHAPTER FOUR

INTENTION

PURPOSE
PATH
FATE
DISCOVERY
CARE-TAKING

PURPOSE

Life is a journey intertwined with a master plan. No matter how big or small, we will need to accomplish or achieve it.

If we acknowledge our life has purpose, we suddenly feel a sense of satisfaction. Our forethought will motivate us to reach our goals and we will watch our progress play out with ambition, motivation, and then accomplishment.

I imagine we all have a purpose aligned for our highest good.

I think we should ask ourselves: are we stepping forward with a clear intent to reach our potential and live inspired? Or are we being stimulated by an event which has happened in the past?

I do understand if you claim your life events have made you who you are today; this is true up to a point. Our memories are a part of who we believe we are, and we tend to construct our lives based on them. If they are significantly positive ones, well that's splendid! If they aren't so great, well, all we can hope for is to honor our fate and the life lesson learned.

Our past or future should not drive our decisions or our actions. They may be linked to an unapparent memory within our emotional, mental or physical self.

Be careful here, as you may have a tendency to invest most of your effort in understanding what has happened, thus prohibiting you from accessing possible new opportunities or igniting the discovery of your soul purpose.

PATH

The patterns of society have been seriously altered in the last few decades, and humanity is living in the midst of many more changes. It is truly amazing to watch the evolution and expansion from over the last 40 years or so with the application of scientific knowledge, modern medicine and a possible plan to travel to Mars in the 21st century. (Really... Mars!)

Regardless of all our advancements, this does not change human nature. There are still many streets, cities, states and countries filled with billions of people; each and every one offers some type of principle.

We are given a name at birth when we enter the world. It is chosen for us.

Our caregivers assist us as children to develop into independent individuals. It is chosen for us

Our food, clothing, and in some cultures, a life partner, is chosen for us.

But accessing our life path occurs on an individual soul-conscious level, revealed by our Higher-Self. It does not live in a memory or in our history, seeking out some form of familiar scenario. It surely does not live in the future, as if we hope to find it one day. And it is definitely not chosen for us by someone else.

We have the opportunity to set any intention based on our life path. To do so, it would be helpful to know our goal, have a clear outlook and create a solid strategy.

As we become closer to our intention, we may notice feelings of joy, praise and happiness, or perhaps thoughts founded in fear, failure or want. If we fail to discover our path, apprehension may be felt, or we may worry about a possible setback. This is only a concept; a fearful storyline which will sabotage your attempt to break free from a limited way of living.

To help your story unfold, I suggest you observe where you have become complacent, resistant or hesitant with moving forward and instead, explore what is unfamiliar.

FATE

Writing the previous paragraphs rekindles memories of my family and our history; especially a relationship I hold dear with my Grandma Bell. I have been told I was her favorite and have inherited her strength and free spirit.

I imagine she struggled with her fate when she lost two young children. I cannot imagine, and wish to never know, the sorrow these events may have caused her in her lifetime. She had shared with me that the aspect of trust was lost somewhere during this tragedy. Sadly, I understand why.

Even so, she continued on, as she was a woman of great courage and resilience, and for me, a great inspiration. I remember one of our many chats we shared; she could not understand this existence, the celebrations or the tribulations of life.

Even though her life was not how she imagined it to be, she comprehended and often reminded me to live fully, to always dance and to never, ever settle for anything other than true love.

———————————

I also recall reading a story linked to Greek mythology about the Fates. It was told that three female goddesses determine the birth and fate of all human life and events.

It would be interesting to believe our destiny is designed by a god or goddess bringing forth events affecting us and our environment; that they are ultimately creating circumstances where we disregard our free will.

Perhaps this is true, as it appears fate has shaped our lives and what is destined will emerge with or without our permission.

I believe at some point when we awaken, especially if we're on a spiritually conscious path, we learn we have little control over the events surrounding us; but we always have self-control and the choice of how we wish to engage with the circumstances.

Perhaps if we choose, we will discover our strength and courage to continue on without the fear of what we cannot understand. We will accept there is a purpose of some sort, even if it is unknown to us. I know our world spins on its axis, best supported when we are founded in love and trust, which is the foundation of all things.

I promise you it is not fear.

DISCOVERY

We are much more powerful than we can ever comprehend. To access our power, it will require seeing every day as brand new.

Learning we are not limited to the Live Line, or compelled to the thoughts of the past and possible future, we begin to experience a serendipity as we step forward onto a path we call our fate. Here we make all we do seem like a dream that has no beginning and no end.

I believe our life starts right where we are. Right now. This moment is the only place we can begin to create an intention. We have permission to revisit our stories. However, only take from them what is in our best interest. Hopefully our wisdom will help us access our Highest Intelligence, while we leave the rest behind.

We must always remember the Higher-Self has chosen a life path filled with change, transformation and the Unknown. On the Live Line, whatever is to come will come whether we like it or not. And that's okay, because being human is to interact, to have a discovery and to observe our adventure.

CARE-TAKING

Rediscovering and realigning the Self is necessary now more than ever.

It is important that we go back to the basics of care-taking by establishing balance and well-being.

Self-care can begin with drinking enough water, making consciously healthy food choices and sleeping at least seven hours a night. Once we establish a healthy foundation, we have the basis to explore who we are and what we wish to experience within our lifetime. A clear intention of our goals will re-establish our commitment; it will motivate us to walk the line we know is a link to our life path.

Your work begins with awareness, and the change you are creating is on a micro level. One day, we will awaken to discover we have transformed and are *Living Aligned*. In the meantime, all we can do is try to understand our optimal choices, practice self-care and live here in the moment.

CHAPTER FIVE

IMPRESSION

🍎

SKETCH
ASSOCIATION
CONDITIONED

SKETCH

An impression is defined in the Aligning program as an isolated event the body and mind holds onto, which is linked to an auditory, visual or olfactory experience stimulating a sensation embedded within the subconscious.

A word, image, scent or even music can trigger memories that will activate our senses. On the spectrum of vast emotional responses, we may choose a state of neutral or an association to excitement/happiness or anxiety/sadness. We all have a personal sketch of our mental, emotional and physical being imprinted. At one time or place, we have experienced a positive or negative charge in the body based on an event, creating a "drawing" of our very own personal memory.

When we recall a memory, we have a form of selective amnesia. We will only remember a fragment of certain memories; that mental sketch of an isolated event we felt moved by in a positive or negative way.

If such an impression has been activated, we may believe the sensation we experience when interacting with a person or the environment is responsible for what we feel. This is not true. The person or situation has not chosen your emotional, mental or physical response. You have.

Selective amnesia has and will alter the actual events that have come to pass. We may not recall the reality of the situation as the fine details dissipate with the lapse of time and the loss of clear memory.

When we are triggered, we can ask ourselves:

- Are we being accountable for *our* thoughts?
- Are we being accountable for *our* feelings?
- Are we being accountable for *our* actions?

We will always have a choice on how to respond. Any thought, feeling or action is the individual's responsibility.

ASSOCIATION

There are so many ways to express ourselves. Without them, we would have a hard time relating to and communicating with each other. Conveniently for us, language has its ground rules on: how to articulate the shapes we call letters; a wave of sound when speech travels through the air to form words; how we are educated based on the definition of these words; and ultimately, the ability to communicate with each other.

Can you remember red construction paper hearts from your childhood? I bet you just formed an image of a heart in your mind.

Now, how perfect is this: when we spell the word H-E-A-R-T, we also remember the shape of a heart. We may recall a paper heart, but all the same, the visual or identification of the word is what we needed to access.

We think of an apple, and believe an apple exists even if there is no physical apple. We simply remembered an apple. In fact, there is a strong possibility that it was the last apple you saw. How the mind and body work to create an impression or word association based on information is a bit different.

Let's use rain as an example:

You've decided to go to the beach.

It rains.

Now, you don't like the rain.

This morning, you thought of rain and you became sad because of your prior experience.

This isn't the brain creating an emotional response; this is the conditioned mind, and yes, they are different. It's that sketch we've created with the thought of rain. The brain has no emotional attachment to your definition; however, it may have an association.

CONDITIONED

Our circle of family, friends and those we look up to shared words with us, then we added an emotional meaning based on what was seen, heard, smelled or felt at the time. We have an intimate relationship with the things that have touched us and memories have been established. Somewhere along our journey of countless experiences, we generated our very own personal definitions within a language.

This is truly amazing—until there is a negative association with something. Many of these events will remain as an impression to create an attachment. Others will move through us, then be released when we take a full inhale and exhale without resistance. When we become surprised, startled or frightened, we will hold our breath in an attempt to protect the body, even if only for a few moments, becoming tense and tight.

We discussed earlier that the vital life force is the breath. If we hold our breath, we become rigid. The vital life force cannot flow through the body. Its full capacity becomes motionless and inflexible. This creates a fear-charged subconscious memory planted somewhere in the body that we access when a similar event occurs in our lifetime. We will respond with the same physical, emotional or mental reaction in the body. We may become angry, feel hurt and isolate ourselves as steps to protect our vulnerability; however, this will only create an unconscious, defensive response toward ourselves or another.

Our reaction is a method of protection against the feelings we do not like. Unfortunately, we are creating a block of some sort, and to block means the vital life force is no longer flowing.

The rise and fall of our actions are based on what we believe is best for ourselves, but most likely linked to a response that resides within an impression. The situation has taken us from our center, leading to an experience of excitement or anxiety.

The mind creates a hindrance that may manifest itself in many ways. We may become obsessed with the events of the past or future. What happened? Why did it happen? What could I have done to change it? Or, we may focus on the future goal, thinking when it is accomplished, we will feel better.

When our vital life force is blocked by the "should haves" or "will bes," we cannot access our true intelligence, which has all the knowledge we will ever need to guide us through the situations we've been presented with.

There is a concept called Nature vs. Nurture. I once read a fascinating article written by Dr. John B. Watson on environmental learning, one of the oldest debates in psychology.

It opens up the curiosity: is perception based on Nature or Nurture?

The theory begins with the question: are we a product of our genes and DNA, or subject to the environmental factors which make us who we are and do what we do? Let's look a little more closely at the difference between the two.

Nature: The genes of each cell in all humans decide the traits of the physical elements of height, hair, eye color and the shape of one's nose. Science is still researching attributes of intelligence, sexual orientation and personality that could be genetic codes in our DNA as well.

Nurture: Behavior influenced by friends, family, life experiences and the environment.

I have my mother's ageless complexion, curly hair and creative side. I have my father's deep brown eyes and love for music. Obviously, I have my curls and my chocolate brown eyes due to my parents' genetic makeup.

My surroundings encouraged my Long Island accent, which I never hear when I speak.

We are educated based on our environment, dressed in the clothing we are given and served the fruit that grows in our gardens.

So, I have a conclusion: we are subjected to, and shaped by, both Nature and Nurture.

CHAPTER SIX

AUTHENTICITY

FREEDOM
INSIGNIFICANT
LIBERATION
DETACHMENT

FREEDOM

When an infant is newly born, he is free to breathe, sleep, smile or cry. He enters life without any form of mental or emotional conditioning. His innocent state of being is allowed to be.

As adults, we have misplaced this natural act of what it means to feel free, exchanging our freedom for agreements to keep a sense of calm in our lives.

In human nature, if we cannot see something, we believe it does not exist. If we no longer feel a connection to something, we may believe it has ceased to exist. If something is lost, we will most likely seek it out. We're searching for something and we don't even know what's missing.

What are we looking for? This very thing we search for lives within us. Obviously we cannot find something we already have. Perhaps we are simply hoping to find the transition from freedom to liberation.

INSIGNIFICANT

I feel the multi-mass media has discovered a connection between the consumer's power of purchasing and the feeling of being significant. It's being utilized in our marketing world to create the illusion that we are insignificant unless we fall captive to the lifestyle they offer for an impossible state of perfection.

I can't recall the last time I watched or listened to commercial television or radio. I made the choice a few years ago to step off the grid. I'm still working on a more simple life, but am happy with the decision to end my relationship with cable television. It's a start. I felt like I was being sold something, mostly due to the abundant advertising. I observed many commercials that spoke to the audience with an air of instant gratification. If we buy this drink, we will lose 25 pounds in a month. If we wear this clothing brand, we will be respected. If we drive this car, we will have status.

I have no problem with having nice things or taking care of ourselves, but not to support an identity. I find it challenging if someone purchases an item because they believe it can buy peace, acceptance or freedom.

LIBERATION

If we are not what we have been told to buy or be, then I think it would be natural for the question "Who Am I?" to arise. This question can throw us off balance if we're not clear about our true Self.

It may feel intimidating to open the door to a psychological state of "Who Am I?" When we take the steps to live free of a past perception about our Self, it may not be easy. Some of us may struggle with the thought that we are at risk of losing a valuable piece of ourselves. We need time to reflect upon our attachments and beliefs, recognizing the things we are willing to trade off as we explore our authentic Self.

The risk you take will be worth it—I promise.

Your willingness to thrive over what is genuine will be all you need to begin the process to live authentically. I hope at this point you have decided your connection to something real is more important than anything else.

It will be a transitional state, almost like crossing a bridge. You'll need to decide if you are willing to leave what you know behind and cross it to discover what is on the other side. It could be the real you, who you have searched for your entire life.

What would be more sad than never meeting the authentic Self would be to create one based on the limited perspective of the stories in which society tells you what you should be.

Nevertheless, I understand if you need a coping method to keep the lower-self in a secure, controlled environment. What has this offered you so far? Have you chosen to live optimally? Are you building the life you imagined?

I would ask yourself these questions over and over. If you are not answering with "yes," you may be missing out on meeting your actual Self.

The journey to liberation begins with acknowledging there is nothing outside of us that offers us freedom, and that we are so much more than what we believe ourselves to be.

DETACHMENT

We must recognize our attachments when recreating the Self, and be willing to release them, allowing no fuss in the mind of what you may lose as you begin to detach.

It is your right to choose what and how to detach, knowing you are not obligated. We always have the ability to choose freely. This is liberation.

Freedom is a powerful expression. A state of complete trust will appear as a form of confidence at times. You may decide to release your story because you have realized you no longer need one. Your authentic Self is enough and you are worthy. When your consciousness rises to this comprehension, a potential transformation will be felt: you are free to choose anything you would like.

Any thought, any word or any action.

You will be free to choose your reaction.

You will be free to be silent.

You are free to do whatever you wish.

Freedom is an internal experience. It lives within us. Once acknowledged, you will rediscover your right to live liberated and achieve the impossible under any circumstances. Even a prisoner who sits in a jail cell can choose to be free in his own mind.

Once liberation is proclaimed, we can be without guilt or attachment.

CHAPTER SEVEN

PEACE

CENTER
CONFLICT
NEUTRAL

CENTER

Visualize a sphere, and within its center resides a state of peace. See a ring of energy surrounding a middle point with the absence of conflict, where no distress, disturbance or suffering exists.

Image 7.1

I believe we confuse peace with peacefulness; they look and sound similar, but they do not feel the same.

Peacefulness is being content or untroubled—the opposing definition of being unpeaceful, which is comparable to agitation or worry.

I've watched people I care about struggle with their feelings just trying to remain calm. It appears they are working very hard to avoid things, perhaps even people, they feel will threaten their tranquil composure. Depending on the situation, I think having a sense of control plays a major role in keeping our emotions in check. Sounds good—I'm all about mastering self-control. But, this doesn't mean a person is experiencing a quiet mind.

Peace lives within us; it is a neutral state where there is no conflict or discord. It may appear still, silent and is definitely impartial. Neutrality helps us remain at the center of all things to observe a 360-degree view of our environment. Here, we have the power of choice. Peace is not prejudice and has no opposite. Some believe it can be attained, but this is not true, because it is what we already have and what we are.

CONFLICT

Our world was created to be a vibrant observation filled with many choices where opposites exist. It is what the human experience consists of. Where there is conflict, life is experienced within an odd balance separated from the whole.

Up/Down

Right/Wrong

East/West

PEACE

Good/Bad

Female/Male

Black/White

Light/Dark

This is the natural state of our world.

Conflict exists within most things we will experience. If there are differences, one side may be "right" and the other is "wrong." This internal struggle is created when believing the side we chose is the correct one; however, it is the challenge and resolution of the conflict that will leave us feeling satisfied. The contrast is an illusion we have embraced as a reality.

The conflict is not the issue. It is the decision we've made to be on the right side and not on the wrong side (according to our own definition).

The need for opposites is vital.

Male and female unite and create life.

The light and dark are one as they exist because of the other. Where the light and dark meet, there is no conflict, split or contrast. The colors black and white merge in the middle and create a gray line. If you observe closely, you may see a hairline fracture that lies at the center of the black and white.

The gray is at the center...it is where peace lives.

NEUTRAL

A few years back, we experienced a disastrous hurricane on Long Island. Many of my friends and colleagues were uprooted when they lost their homes to massive flooding. It was a devastating event that brought many challenging times. Since then, many have walked away from their homes due to the excessive damage. They are in my thoughts with peace.

Living near the water on the south shore of the island, I was concerned about how the storm would affect my family. We were fortunate, as my home had only lost electricity for about 12 hours.

I recall being at the mercy of Mother Nature with her 80mph winds and rain. All I could do was make sure we had enough water, batteries and candles. There is no denying the first few hours of the storm against our large front window filled me with an underlying anxiety.

After collecting my thoughts, I remembered we were safe. I returned to my center and I had an insight: my life is pretty convenient with lights, gas and running water.

What would happen if I lost this? Am I prepared to live merely with the basics for a few hours, a week or maybe for the rest of my days? Then I remembered: I have all I need. I brought myself back to a neutral state.

PEACE

Positive goals will stimulate us to feel a heightened state of excitement, happiness, peace or accomplishment. Usually this is done from the need to become happy or to gain something.

This is what some believe it is to feel alive.

We would never wish to be sad or angry, but throughout life we will feel anxious, frightened, neglected or that we have failed at one time or another.

This is also what some believe is to feel alive.

The rise and fall of our actions are based on what we believe is best. The situation has taken us from our center, leading to an experience of excitement or anxiety. By returning to a space of neutral, we can restore our sense of peace.

CHAPTER EIGHT

GOOD & BAD

JUDGMENT

REALITY

THRIVE

JUDGMENT

I've come to a conclusion that may seem naïve to many. I believe most people have a compassionate heart with good intentions of doing their best. I think society tries to live a decent life based on the individual belief of what it may mean to be a good person. I am aware not everyone thinks like me.

What is good for one person may be bad for another. We have opinions which may vary as we watch someone make a choice to do something good, believing this will make them a good person. That very same person may make what we believe is a bad choice; are they now a bad person?

A judgment based on what you believe does not give you permission to sit on a pedestal. This is because this illusion is based on your perception. The "I am good and he is bad" concept will keep you locked into your limited belief system, ultimately leading to adversity for yourself and the party involved.

We live in a diverse world with many human beings of different shapes, colors and sizes. Some have relationships with men and others with women. They are multi-cultural and have many religious practices. Here in America, we have our way of doing things. We need not be intimidated by what appears different. This is neither good nor bad. It simply is.

My family is an old fashioned one. They are close-knit, simple folk who like to cook, eat and spend time with the people they love. My parents sternly expressed their perspective of how their children should be raised. They established what they believed was good and bad for me and my siblings based on an authoritarian discipline.

In my younger years, we did not talk back to elders in the family. We were in bed by 9pm on school nights and no dessert was allowed before dinner. Resisting their rules would have led to terrible consequences, like having no TV or playdates, or even being yelled at. As we grew older, the curfew was always 10pm, and there was no dating outside our cultural belief system. Looking back now, of course it was not as strict as I thought. In fact, my cousins on my dad's side had a much more difficult time than I did.

The order my parents created was necessary to keep life as they knew it controlled and regulated, and of course, to protect us from mischief or being harmed.

I'm sure most parents do this to keep their children and beliefs safe.

REALITY

I recall in my adolescence deciding to explore Buddhism. I suppose my mother was silently unsettled by seeing me read these articles and books on eastern philosophy. Once she stared at me oddly and asked, "Are you a Buddhist now?" I suppose the shiny silver pendant of Buddha I wore for a few months caught her eye. She never said it was bad, but the facial expressions and body language defined it as not good.

GOOD AND BAD

Considering my mother and her religious beliefs based in Catholicism, someone practicing a Protestant religion would think my mother's beliefs were bad and theirs were good.

I imagine an individual has their beliefs and feels righteous about their practices.

I think most of the things we do not understand may make us feel uncomfortable. You might need to contemplate this one, as it may be challenging to understand and accept the concept. (It was for me in the beginning of my practice.) Only in the human experience can we have the good and bad opinion; there is no good or bad within the collective process of the Universal Consciousness. We are one in our integrity. We are whole.

There is no opposite or separation; however, within the small mind, we tend to create a conflict about one or the other.

When we separate ourselves with a split concept, we become prejudiced, restricted and limited. When we judge another, it is linked to our conditioning, which is rooted in an agreement we did not decide for ourselves.

When an opinion or judgment is expressed, inquiry is necessary. We must ask ourselves if it is founded in fact or fiction.

Fact: based in truth, reality.

Fiction: based on an individual's perception.

Please know I am aware of the favorable and opposing aspects in life. I am fully conscious of the positive and negative events unfolding in our world. I am strongly averse to someone's wrongdoing. However, the point I am stressing is that we cannot create an alliance within a fictional state of mind; it must be based on what is factual.

When we choose to live within the scope of reality, opinions and judgments linked to belief systems of what is good and bad will hold no power over you.

THRIVE

Let's do an exercise.

The good and bad play a role in what we feel and will influence the fundamental choices we make. When you are feeling a little adventurous, take a break from reading and grab a pen and an unlined piece of paper.

Write a line across the top and a line down the center. On the left, write the word "good," and on the right side, write the word "bad."

Under the good column, jot down five things you believe are "good" aspects of your life or in the world. Under the "bad" column, add five things you believe are "bad" aspects of your life or in the world.

Stop and take a deep breath. Now cross out the word "good." Then cross out the word "bad."

Now, really take a look at what you wrote. What do we have, but a few lines and a bunch of words you are attached to that are the good and bad in your world?

Collectively-speaking, it is possible that what you wrote is really "bad," like homelessness or murder. And of course, many would approve of being compassionate or support conscious environmental actions.

I understand and respect this, and I agree. What I want to point out is the need to awaken our awareness to an attachment based on our need to thrive or strive for what is good and bad based solely on an opinion.

Thrive: When we thrive, we grow or develop based on the guidance of the Higher-Self. We feel motivated and all things flow naturally. We seek to flourish because the intention is not lost in reaching the goal; it is placed on being in peace.

Strive: This shows great effort to achieve. Our only focus is to obtain something and it may involve a struggle, if necessary. It is our desire on the Live Line which motivates us. It also may feel challenging to reach the goal.

It could be helpful to reflect upon on your good and bad columns and recognize what evokes your emotional reactions. Discovering what topics you have a strong attachment to just may be where you're invested.

It requires so much time and energy to strive. It is truly an unnecessary battle to live the "good" life. We should not sacrifice our peace and authenticity to uphold the quality of life that we may or may not desire. Instead, let's thrive and approach our lives patiently. Simply being a kind, compassionate person would be a great start.

CHAPTER NINE
EIGHT SECOND RULE

REVELATION
ANANDA
STILLNESS
8-SECONDS
ESR

REVELATION

I will share a little something about myself: I'm a perfectionist. I love drawing with fine line markers, my handbag almost always matches my boots and I've been told I tend to be a bit controlling at times. When it comes to my personal and work life, I need this sense of order to create structure as I accomplish my "to do" list for the day.

I'm pretty sure I didn't always see my own character traits. I suppose it's why I have certain people in my life I trust, so they can call me out when needed (I'm smiling).

I remember wanting to take care of my family, my friends and whomever I thought needed some sort of support. It guess it comes with the territory of being an intuitive life coach.

This took a bit of effort on my behalf to recognize I wasn't always taking care of myself. It dawned on me: maybe the person I was tending to did not want to be taken care of. It was possible the party did not want to change anything. Maybe they wanted to figure it out on their own, or they didn't really give a damn. I realized how rigid my actions were, holding on to what I believed was a part of my personality. I believed I had no bad traits. I never smoked, ate pretty healthy and was a compassionate person—plus I was a good daughter and friend.

At all times, I was living in what was my truth. I imagine most people feel they are, until something happens to make them question their commitments and actions, or what they believe to be the truth.

While traveling one winter out West, I thought I would add a few
days to my journey and visit my sister in California.

My stay with her was eventful on many levels, as we ventured out
for a road trip to Santa Barbara. The Pacific Ocean and lunch were
perfect; however, we had a disagreement.

Somewhere in between what was left of our mint tea and my
sister driving back to Los Angeles, we salvaged our time together
before my flight back to New York. She shared, "I know you mean
well, but I want to figure this one out on my own."

I felt uncomfortable and unsettled. I was aware of the feeling I'd
experienced so many times before...conflict. I knew my approach
to my sister, and to many other aspects of my life, would need
to change. My mind was running like a wild horse carrying
saddlebags filled with questions on how. I thought if I could find a
quiet space and stop multi-tasking in my mind, maybe an answer
would magically appear.

How do I change something about myself if I'm unaware I'm even
doing such a thing? What was I doing wrong?

I watched the clouds dance from my aisle seat for what I'm sure
was more than eight seconds and realized a tough lesson. I heard
her statement, and I acknowledged it.

I had to let her go.

She was not my responsibility. I needed to step back.

I knew she would make the best decision for herself.

ANANDA

One late spring over a decade ago, I attended a silent retreat in upstate New York at Ananda Ashram. Ananda means extreme happiness, bliss and all that good stuff. Definitely a sign of good things to come.

The weekend venture offered a clean, sunlit-filled dorm room I shared with five women. The light blue walls were the same color as the comforter which appeared cozy enough to help me feel at ease. The three days would include vegetarian meals and assorted teas daily at no additional cost. My view of the lake from the large bay window on the second floor was breathtaking. I felt at peace, although a little concerned about how I could not speak for the next 60 hours.

Upon my arrival, I was given a round orange pin with bright blue writing, "Being Silent" boldly written at its center. I decided to pin it on my left side as I headed to the dining hall. I walked down a steep hill requiring a bit of effort. Immediately, I heard my own voice ring in my head and say, "Really, this is so steep; I don't want to do this."

I was surprised with the underlying tone of frustration. After what felt like a short hike, I arrived at the dining hall and it was filled with men and women wearing round orange pins with nowhere to sit.

Again, I heard the voice in my head say, "I can't believe this."

This inner dialogue we have within ourselves is something we do unconsciously. The mind jumps around without any form of order, from whining about a steep hill to "I want birthday cake."

The choice to not speak that weekend did not mean my mind shut off. It was indeed stirring, juggling all of the events of life in that one moment.

My mind's focus was on what I needed to do, and what I didn't want to do.

What I did do, and what I didn't do.

What they did to me, and what I did to them.

What they said, and what I would say.

How will it happen? I want to know right now!

STILLNESS

I appeared silent at my retreat; however, I was not. I did notice there was a stillness in my breath when I was trying to work out the clutter in my mind (thank goodness!).

After dinner, the group and I walked down toward the lake, and then attended a fire ceremony. The fire, mantra and breathwork did me good. Sitting with the warmth of the flames, I initiated several deep inhales, which enabled me to escape the confinement of my scattered thoughts. This helped me remember it was all in my mind. When I exhaled, I realized it was just a story I was creating.

Stillness and breath were my way to quiet the chatter in my mind.

Sitting in meditation, I would breathe and be still. I would have a hurtful thought of someone I felt had broken my heart; I would breathe and be still. I felt anger about something someone said; I would breathe deeply and be still. The times I did not choose to breathe deeply and be still, I didn't like my thoughts, what I felt or what I did.

The two-hour drive home on Route I-87 helped me process the events of this simple, yet amazing discovery...stillness. I chose to remain silent for the rest of my drive home. I turned on the radio and contemplated if singing at the top of my lungs would count as speaking.

I came to realize soon after my time at Ananda that I could not answer my mind's random statements and thoughts with no start or end.

The mind likes to be busy thinking to fill the void of silence. It is not searching for anything other than to avoid the things it cannot understand, like the Unknown.

8-SECONDS

In the stillness near the Ananda Lake, I created the Eight Second Rule. The effortless act of a four-second inhale and a four-second exhale can change the vibration of our entire being. As

I progressed in my practice, I would breathe, pause and decide if I liked the thought or not. The thoughts I did not like I let go of by not focusing in on them. Soon after, I noticed a change in my response. I chose the thoughts I would engage with, and they would flow in and out of my mind and no longer had power over me or my choices.

I began to feel different. I no longer viewed myself as a guide, a victim or a survivor, but rather as an individual empowered to make healthy and clear decisions. Of course, this would alter the way I reacted to my surroundings, and then others also changed the way they responded. Observing what was happening within myself was powerful, as it awakened an awareness not to silence, but to stillness.

In the silence there is no void of sound; it is that I am still as sound happens.

Image 9.1

EIGHT SECOND BREATH

INHALE
4 SECONDS

EXHALE
4 SECONDS

ESR

So how it works is pretty simple. When you have a thought that evokes an emotion—positive or negative—you will inhale four seconds and then exhale four seconds before engaging or responding to what is going on in your mind. *Image 9.1* on the left reflects this process.

The timeline may feel like an eternity, but it will bring mindfulness to your feelings and thoughts. You should ask yourself: are your thoughts based on what is factual or merely an emotional rise of excitement or anxiety? This is where we make the choice and create the next moment; where we remain clear-minded when interacting with life.

It can be cumbersome to do the Eight Second Rule ("ESR") with another person; however, we can learn something about our relationships, the environment and why we feel so intense about one's actions and care little about another's.

I noticed when I chose not to use the ESR with another, I would feel anxious and unconscious feelings would rise up. In no way did I want to feel uncomfortable or make another feel uneasy.

It was super important that I took care of my needs and respected others at the same time. I did realize when utilizing the ESR, it was not my responsibility to take care of anyone. I know that may sound harsh, but in the beginning of the work, it took great effort to not judge myself or another when someone did not do or say what I wanted.

It was transformative when I aligned with my breath instead of reacting. The awareness of how my mind would become worked up was a great eye-opener for me. The Eight Second Rule helped me to engage in a neutral way; to not be emotionally reactive and to become a better listener. Applying the ESR when we interact with another can be insightful and liberating. If a person stimulates a feeling to make you feel happy or sad, instead of reacting, you inhale then exhale before you respond.

When someone asks you a question, wait the eight seconds. The space between the question and answer may be seriously awkward; but it doesn't always need to be a full eight seconds. In the beginning, it could be a two or three second process.

I suggest practicing with family and friends; you can always share your intention for the exercise after you're done, or even experience it together.

Let's do an ESR exercise.

Sit in a comfortable chair with your feet grounded on the floor. Take three full breaths and release any tension in the body.

When a thought pops up, before choosing to hold on to it, take a full four-second inhale and a full four-second exhale. You can

CHAPTER TEN

ENLIGHTENED

INSPIRED
ENLIGHTENMENT
FAITH
WEAKENED
HEALING
TEMPORARY
GRACEFULLY

INSPIRED

Many masters have declared our intention is to be at peace and reach enlightenment. Teachers from many continents extend their message with the intent to define what it means to live in this heightened state of existence.

I've been inspired by so many: Jiddu Krishnamurti, Byron Katie Mitchell and his Holiness, the Dalai Lama. I only mention a few, as there are so many whom have moved me with their guidance and wisdom.

My discovery of the Old Master, Lao-Tzu, a Chinese philosopher, helped accelerate my shift to *Living Aligned*. It is said he may have lived before the 5th century, leaving behind the sacred writing of *The Tao Te Ching*. My reading of the ancient text inspired my belief that enlightenment is possible in our lifetime.

ENLIGHTENMENT

What is enlightenment?

- Comprehension
- Detachment
- Compassion
- Awareness
- Insight
- Liberation
- Integrity
- Gratitude
- Peace

Most people believe if we do the work and become enlightened we'll be rewarded: a concept linked to an exception. Some believe if we practice meditation, celibacy or take a vow of silence, it will help us reconnect to the source. Suddenly, our lives will miraculously appear flawless and our troubles will fall away as we emerge onto the one and only path to the ultimate state of existence.

I don't think it really works that way. Perhaps a diligent practice of a daily meditation is a good place to start, though.

We're not living on a mountain top or in a temple; we co-exist and are required to associate with other beings on this planet. Plus, our families, financial issues and health concerns will most likely override our commitment to a yoga class.

Personally, I have chosen a life with the responsibility of a child to feed, clothe and love. I do not foresee leaving this behind any time soon, nor do I want to do so. However, I am willing to commit to my own path. No matter how slow the process, I will remain focused while I live here in this modern world of social media, skinny jeans and coffee at every corner.

Remember the masters may have been inspired young, met a great mystic along the way or endured some form of suffering or chaos which led to their enlightenment. I could continue to tell countless stories of what inspired another's path. Unfortunately, this will not lead you nor I to understand what it is to be enlightened; it cannot be discussed or read—it can only be experienced.

FAITH

I think most people have dreams and big plans for their life: to find a fulfilling career, fall in love or travel to foreign lands.

It's possible the Universe has planned something else for you. Maybe, we are not where we thought we would be...

We will question the events of our lives as the body fails us with its aches, pains and aging process. It is impossible to invest our energies into a career if there is no job to go to, and we should never collapse into a lover even if he or she offers some type of false security.

The circumstances of life cause us to question and create an internal struggle with what is happening in the present moment. I understand if we need answers; we're wrestling with this feeling of uncertainty and hoping things will turn out the way we would like, or at least for the best.

Thank goodness everything changes, for change is one of the most perpetual things we will experience in life. It allows us to try again, to start over and even offers the option to reinvent ourselves.

Many of us are uneasy with altering the way things are simply because the circumstance is unknown to us. Change, transition or transformation is inevitable at one point in our career and relationships, and even the Self will go through some form of metamorphosis. If you have reached this stage, it is possible your perception of reality is slowly being stripped away, so even the basic elements of comfort have been removed.

In times of transformation, there are no distractions to rescue us or co-dependent resources to turn to as we once did. Life happens, and we really do not have much control over the situation. I'm sure it will most likely override what we imagine it could offer.

Unfortunately, the pleasure of an optimistic practice to keep us connected to our primary nature during such transitions may be lost in daily responsibilities and obligations.

I understand it is not everyone's destiny to live as an enlightened master, new ager or a yogi. But we still must become accountable for the care-taking of ourselves; not only to create a healthier lifestyle, but to also step away from someone that does not respect us, or simply to give ourselves permission to rest.

When the body feels weak, we wonder if the situation will ever end. The internal knowledge of our basic needs being met seems to disappear. In a weakened state, we will attempt to replace information with some sort of hope that things will get better. Caution is advised here, as the term "I hope" is linked to a maybe. "I hope" is a 50% chance it can go either way.

What we need is to find our faith once more, making our emotional and spiritual well being a priority during the times of doubt. When we are aligned with our faith, we are living assured—100% certain we will prevail. When things change, we can access our ability to trust in ourselves and have courage to make the necessary adjustments in our favor.

WEAKENED

"When The Body Feels Weak"

At this point in my life, I can speak clearly without uncertainty. I trust the circumstances of my life are unfolding just right as I am raising my daughter with ease. I'm feeling a bit of financial pressure; however, I am healthy and training for a 5k this fall.

When my body feels strong, I can conquer any diversion. I feel fully capable and resilient to continue on through any storm. When the body feels weak—hurting physically, mentally or emotionally—this is easier said than done.

In the past, when I experienced a weakened state, I could hear the negative thoughts one at a time begin to pile at the center of my mind during challenging times. The hows and whys made my head and body hurt, becoming seduced by memories of where hopelessness lived.

This pain was a reminder of something that lived in the body, triggered by the current event. I could not recall mentally what had upset me. I could not think straight. All I wanted to do was eat, sleep and cry. The disturbance isolated me and kept me from the people and places whom could shed light on my suffering.

HEALING

The body has the ability to regenerate itself. For example, when the flesh has been damaged, the wound will begin to heal before we acknowledge there has been an injury. In time, it will be healed and return to a healthy state. If the old wound remains untended, we will need assistance to remove what stands in the way so it may heal completely.

A thought or feeling which may be linked to a negative timeline in your life is basically the same, whether experienced mentally or emotionally. These wounds are most challenging to heal because we cannot see them or understand the method to heal them.

When we have pain, we feel pain. Not much new about this statement. The pain is helping us to be aware that something has gone awry, like a fever arising with chills in an unhealthy body. The fever attempting to burn away bacteria can be an uncomfortable experience; however, we know the body is doing what it must to fight the disease and return to an optimal state.

Releasing negative thoughts and feelings are similar. We may feel uncomfortable as the association rises to the surface of our emotional or mental state.

We will need to rest, create balance and allow the natural flow of vital life force to move through the physical, mental, emotional and spiritual body to heal.

The vital life force is like running water: it flows and is always moving. When our breath is not moving, we can imagine a block has been created. Similar to water sitting in a glass for too long, it will become murky and smell downright nasty. If left there, it will it begin to evaporate and leave a ring of residue inside the glass.

This may occur within the emotional or mental body because we hold on too tightly to our story due to fear or suffering.

TEMPORARY

I really don't think anyone wants to feel awkward, strained, anxious or in pain, which is why most people tend to preserve their vulnerability. Praise or protection will pop up when we need to feel better about ourselves and create a temporary form of security to feel balanced once more.

- **Praise:** the desire of seeking approval or admiration.
- **Protection:** to prevent suffering, harm or injury.

The mind will produce an illusion of preservation and relief by taking steps based on our beliefs by reaching for food, a drug, shopping or even a relationship. Other distractions we may not recognize that will help us cope or feel better could be overworking, television or even music.

Basically, we are avoiding the feelings we do not want to surface. When the body feels weak, our attention needs to be on allowing the unconscious feeling(s) to surface.

Remember, any feelings that arise are not permanent; it is only our conditioned thoughts which have made it appear so. Any recurring thoughts are responding to what we have accessed on an unconscious level.

The body has its comforts and we need them at times. However, we will need to have our comfort zone rocked to recognize what will help us to heal. I have no doubt the struggle is very real, but we must challenge our belief system and observe the daily feelings that arise when we feel weak, when we do not get what we want or when we feel sad. It is then we can accept our circumstances and begin to explore what is beyond the surface and discover the tools to recreate our lives based on what is genuine.

A few things we must consider:

- During times of weakness, we cannot isolate the Self; we must reach out to a support system of family, friends or a facilitator who can listen or offer guidance.

- Care-taking is essential; we must provide the basic needs of rest, proper nourishment and a clear mind.

- Our co-dependence on our so-called reality must be confronted so that we may find another option beyond what we believe is suffering.

- We can never give up. We must always go on.

All things here on the Earth plane are for a little while: a day, a decade or perhaps a lifetime. At times it will appear as though we will wander blindly. For most, it will be a short walk. For some of us, it will require endurance and investing the little energy we have left to rediscover the means to heal.

Acknowledging that our experiences are temporary will help us deal with life events one day at a time.

GRACEFULLY

The answers are within us, perhaps hiding at the very bottom of the weakness, pain and suffering.

Today, we will choose to gracefully dive deep into this void of our weakened state. Only today, and then we will rest.

My wish for you: when tomorrow comes, you will stare into the face of the hurt and acknowledge, "I am not this. I am something much more than this." It will awaken something within you...it will be peace.

Peace is much more powerful than any tragedy or trauma we have experienced.

No matter how often we lose our way, we will return to peace, time and time again, here in the body and on the elemental plane where the Higher-Self resides. This simple comprehension will adjust our frequency so that a balance of the physical and spiritual plane will occur. What we truly need will ripple outward and onward.

Somewhere, somehow it will have a positive effect on our lives. Realizing that the experience was only here to teach us is where we begin to accelerate the shift to enlightenment.

CHAPTER ELEVEN

TRANSFORMATION

DARK
UNKNOWN
CHANCE

DARK

I recall it was a cloudy Sunday morning on December 10th. I believe there was a lunar eclipse around 9:30am. I felt deeply distraught in a state of sadness I had never known. This heaviness I felt lingered for days, weeks and then months. I have felt sad or angry at one point or another; however, this was an intense, unfamiliar emotion of hopelessness, outrage and uncertainty.

It was time to reflect on what could be the possible cause. I knew there was a risk of stepping into emotions I was not ready for or could not control. Despite my hesitation, I decided to explore this deeper.

I sat in meditation as I have so many times before, supported by the upright wooden chair of my dining table, a blanket to override the cold draft from the kitchen windows and several crystals. After several attempts of soul journey work, I found a bit of clarity...I discovered I needed to embrace the dark.

The idea brought up a streak of unconscious emotions and left me feeling restless, but I knew I had to illuminate this space and find a balance between the light and dark.

I would need to plan an elaborate, advanced approach to my spiritual maturity; a simple way to resist or perhaps accept the fear to discover the light within.

UNKNOWN

That winter changed me, I think forever. The bitter cold winds and short days took my focus away from the everyday routine as I discovered the dark. How appropriate winter solstice brings us the shortest period of daylight and the longest night of the year.

The solstice is a powerful time, as it offers us the opportunity to review the lessons we have learned in the last 12 months. We can focus on what will we take and what we are willing to leave behind.

I am not sure about the rest of the world, but the darkness is not one of my favorite places to be, though I can tolerate it if needed. The darkness is almost like the nightmare horror flicks created in the 1980's, with their homespun special effects of murky shadows, wickedness and scary stuff.

The Dark is different; it is the void of complete instruction, knowledge and expectation. I will call it the Unknown, a place where anything could happen, and most likely, we can never prepare for.

Early on in life, I would think of the Unknown and I felt a bit of anxiety—an uneasy feeling at the bottom of my belly. I remember the day I chose to rid my life of this fearful definition. Luckily, I latched on to a belief I read somewhere in one of the books that still sits on the floor near my nightstand. It was something along the lines of: "We are one with the Universe."

I welcomed the statement and felt compelled to acknowledge somehow all was well. I knew in the deepest part of my soul I had always been guided by a prominent power. I still needed to accept this apprehensive and uncomfortable place we face everyday when the sun sets, when we close our eyes or when we are unsure of what the next day will bring.

It's important that we define the Dark/Unknown as referred to in the Aligning Method:

* Known

* Unknown

* Unknowable

Known: The Known is right here in front of you. It is what you see and what you remember. The Known transforms into accessible knowledge. We have the ability to develop a vast encyclopedia we can tap into as we think, feel and act.

Unknown: The Unknown is like the dark where we should not be frightened. The dark is the void of all you know, but we should not let it intimidate us. The Unknown holds innovation, timelessness and possibility of the future. It is unseen in this very moment.

We will need to separate the association of a fearful darkness and the Unknown, as they are not the same.

Image 11.1 on the following page represents this.

Image 11.1

INNOVATION
UNKNOWN
INFINITE

The Unknown is something you just haven't figured out yet. We will use a bedroom in the dark as an example of the Unknown. We know where the bed and nightstand are, and right there is where the lamp awaits to be turned on. There is no risk of falling to our death; though perhaps we may trip over the book left on the floor as we make our way to the nightstand. That book or falling is not unlike a certain life event that pops up to challenge us on our path.

Unknowable: This is simple. It is none of our business.

The Unknowable is not for you or I to know. If we stumbled upon this information, it could be played out like a time traveler's story creating a butterfly effect: the impact could alter the alignment with your life path and the repercussions could create a paradox in our timeline.

An extremely rare opportunity may arise to reveal what is Unknowable, but again, it is not for us know.

CHANCE

Close your eyes. Really stop reading and close them. Okay, you might have had a passing thought, but ultimately your mind should appear pretty clear, creating a space where we cannot be stimulated by what we perceive outside the Self, or our limited reality.

Being in the dark gives us the opportunity to embrace this complete unconditional, unpredictable and limitless place. For the Higher-Self, it is a lucid, solid foundation it can stand on, moving freely to explore the realm of Infinite Possibilities. A comprehension of Right-Action, visions, dreams and random choices are abundant and infinitely constant at any point when our eyes are closed.

The information cannot be accessed through knowledge, so thinking will not help us; only what we feel at the Heart Center can be our guide. Imagine the spontaneous opportunity that is brand new and undiscovered waiting for you.

I feel fortunate. A few winters had passed and a spark finally occurred. I found the link—a thread between dark and light, the yin and yang, the good and the bad—where all things meet and become one. I discovered many things during the time I spent within the Unknown. However, I had one important realization: we cannot provide for the Self what we cannot see.

A little cognitive twist in our perception is needed so we may see things differently. Transform your belief of a risk into a chance— because we believe taking chances is much safer than taking a risk. It will help the mind rest and release fear for a little while to see unpredictability as an opportunity and allow us to live life without a rehearsal.

I have said many times: if we knew we were safe with all of our actions, we would most likely choose differently.

I offer a bit of advice: live spontaneously. Plan something new and adventurous. Accept all experiences have some purpose in our life, even though the outcome cannot be comprehended in the moment.

TRANSFORMATION

The focus must be on going within to find our internal light, so that darkness, sorrow or fear will never overcome you. And that little ole' light that shines brightly within us will illuminate our path out of the darkness, as well as inspire others to shed their light onto the world we live in.

PART III

LIVING ALIGNED

CHAPTER TWELVE

MEDITATION

CLARITY
MUSE
WAVES
ALPHA

CLARITY

Living an extraordinary life begins with being balanced, awake and aware, and includes having clarity. It is also wise to be knowledgeable of the facts and make decisions based on a good gut feeling. Life is one decision after another. It helps that the universe provides signs that may offer insight into what could lead to the most excellent choices.

If we lose this clear state, our intelligence and intuition may not appear as pronounced. Clarity is essential in helping us to easily interpret any given situation in our lives. We are conscious of how to order a meal, set an alarm and make our way to work.

It's so simple—we trust our process, because making a decision when our mind is sharp is like speaking or walking; if you are fluent in a language you speak, or if you know how to walk, you simply take a step. We proceed forward without any form of hesitation, irrelevant of what the consequences may be.

Misplacing this important connection can lead to feeling unsure, confused or anxious. The beginning stages of doubt will cast a spell of feeling lost, overriding our intelligence that holds the knowledge we need to access to make healthy choices.

When we feel lost, we may seek advice from an outside source; however, only a few close to us will be able to help us identify our true needs. People will offer what they think is best for us, but it is important to remember that it's their perspective—someone else's point of view linked to their own personal opinion or judgment. It is not our own intuitive intelligence.

We all have this vital resource to make life-altering decisions, or even simple ones, like merely choosing if we should date that cute girl or boy.

My conclusion: clarity helps us access our intelligence and intuition.

MUSE

It's obvious our personal decision-making will create the foundation for what will transpire in our lives.

In my early twenties, a friend found it amusing when I shared I had much of the same questions as she did. How odd she thought it sounded, that an intuitive like myself, who guided others to make the most pivotal choices in their lives, was dealing with similar drama. My debate would almost always arise as I began a new romantic relationship. The question of, "Is he the one?" would creep up as feelings began developing for the person.

It took a few years to discover my muse, as I was engrossed by the emotionally-driven mind wanting to understand what would happen next in the relationship. My clarity would be drowned out by the rush of feelings for the potential new love.

It was paramount for me to remain clear and access my intuitive voice during these times of emotional attachment and co-dependency.

But how?

I began observing what was different between the time before and after conducting a meeting with a client. I was straightforward—no fuss or mind chatter—and felt absolutely zero doubt. I recognized I left my life's issues outside the studio. I was neutral, clear and centered. Morning caffeine was forbidden. Plus, I made time each morning to meditate. I was completely objective during the sessions. I felt connected!

These steps were unconsciously integrated within the start of each work day. The pre-session exercises led me to discover the experience of clarity, a connectedness with the client and myself.

To replicate this sense of lucidity in my personal life, it was evident that caffeine would need to be limited, and a morning or evening meditation would become a necessary part of my daily schedule. I started to journal my experiences. I wanted to keep track of how, if in any way, it would alter my daily routine. I started noticing I was not as attached to my emotions, and my problem solving had strengthened. I knew I had stumbled upon something intense, yet I could not quite explain it.

WAVES

My personality wants to know the root cause of most things, what makes them tick and move or do what they do. I've asked many questions and read so many books on the topics which interest me. Honestly, I believe my curiosity has assisted with articulating my life's work. The need to understand how I was accessing an intuitive state led to the discovery of a theory called brain waves.

I was excited!

The comprehension of how the brain and its frequencies worked as a whole defined what I was doing. I had found my answer—I was accessing the Alpha brain wave. Before I go further, let's break down a few key brain wave definitions.

- **Brain Wave**: an electrical impulse in the brain
- **Beta**: awaken/alert
- **Alpha:** rest/intuition
- **Theta:** dream/healing
- **Delta**: deep sleep/dreamless
- **Gamma:** higher perception

I cannot claim I understand the depth of the human brain, as I believe most people will agree it is magnificent and mysterious. I do know it resides at the vertex of the body in the skull. It works together with the central nervous system to control how we function in the body. It is complex and said we use less than 10 percent of its capacity. Communication between brain and body happens at lightning speed.

It is fierce and powerful!

The movement of my fingers on the keys of my laptop as I'm writing is happening super fast. Not to mention the creation of other cool stuff, like our senses being stimulated at the same time: smell, vision, hearing—and we can't forget about feeling!

ALPHA

Dr. Hans Berger, the inventor of electroencephalography (also known as the EEG), was able to detect electrical activity in the human brain sometime in the 1920's. Dr. Berger discovered the Alpha brain wave, which emerges from the occipital lobe and resides at the back of the head. In honor of him, it is called the Berger's wave.

Our brain is made of neurons, which are brain cells. It is said we have lots of them—in fact, billions. They communicate electrically with each other and will change depending on what the person is doing. The brain waves and frequency will react differently when a person is awake, asleep, stressed or calm. The Alpha brain wave is accessed during wakeful relaxation with closed eyes.

Every living person will experience Beta brain wave, as it is our waking state, as well as Delta brain wave, which is deep, dreamless sleep.

The key here is to be in Beta brain wave without multi-tasking, having anxiety or being under stress. If we remain relaxed at our center, we can access Alpha brain wave by merely closing our eyes.

CHAPTER THIRTEEN

MIND-MOTION-MOVEMENT METHOD

MMM
MIND
OBSERVER
THOUGHT
MOTION
MOVEMENT
PATIENCE

MMM

All men, women and children experience the cognitive act of consciously having thoughts. They use observation to make sense of their surroundings and the world. Thoughts transition into thinking, which is interpreted into an understanding of the environment, desires, attachments, intentions, memory and/or imagination. We can further break this process down as *Image 13.1* demonstrates.

Image 13.1

MIND /THINK
MOTION /FEEL
MOVEMENT /ACT

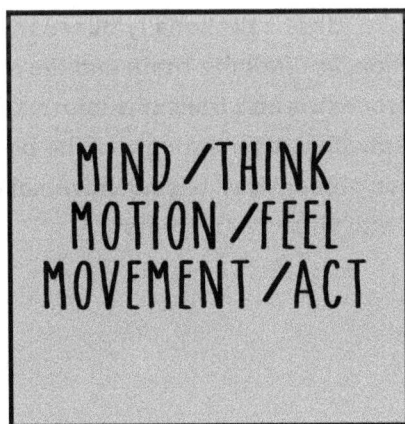

The Mind: the conscious state where one thinks; is aware of the world and accesses knowledge to come to a conclusion.

The Motion: a frequency or force of energy moving within the human body; is transparent and cannot be seen, although can be felt.

The Movement: an act of decision-making or a position decided by the mind or motion.

We are naturally predisposed to a Mind-Motion-Movement process, but our goal is to work towards a Motion-Movement-Mind one. Let's discuss how it all works further.

MIND

The Mind ("to Think") is filled with many memories, stories, beliefs, opinions and ideas. I personally question the mind/brain and body connection, as I feel the brain and the mind are not the same. The brain processes and transmits information through electrical and chemical signals throughout the body. The mind does not, and in our present day, has no universal definition. But, we can start here with what it can create:

•   Ideas

•   Concepts

•   Thoughts

To our disadvantage, the process of thinking has become our first response, replacing possible intuitive feedback. Thinking is a conceptual process which will help us mentally comprehend and come to a conclusion based solely on our perspective. It possibly leads us to opposing what is actually based in reality, misaligning with the facts relevant to the circumstance. We need to integrate the process to work with our mind so that it supports us without blocking our intuitive state.

OBSERVER

The mind is a planner. It wants to know things. It wants to understand things. The mind anticipates: Step one. Step two. Step three. It makes sense to take the steps necessary to reach the goal on the linear line.

Are we observing life based on our repetitive perception to come to a rational decision, or seeing things in a new light? As opposed to the Mind/to Think, the Motion/to Feel is completely random, spontaneous and has no order.

I suggest we try to bridge them to experience the events of our day with a little wonderment, as if for the first time.

Meditation is critical for our thoughts to resist the temptation of patterned thinking. Become an observer to examine and contemplate your emotional and mental reaction. It is important that what we think does not create our reality.

When meditating, if a thought should arise, it should be acknowledged and released with the support of the Eight Second Rule and the breath: a four second inhale as a thought appears, and the four-second exhale, repeated as needed to allow the thought to dissipate.

We then become the spectator, the witness; a person who notices. We remain the observer of the mind's patterns and create an awareness that we are more than just our thoughts, which may or may not be based in reality.

THOUGHT

When a thought appears, we have a choice: will it become a pattern of thinking or simply fleeting?

Allowing the thought to become a repetitive behavior can be very distracting and may propel us to move from one extreme to another. Here, we lose the present moment, which we know is essential for remaining Aligned.

A thought must move in and out of our stream of consciousness. Imagine our thinking process as creating a dense, invisible box surrounding the body. We can visualize the box as a suit of armor made of cast iron metal. It appears heavy and burdensome, similar to most of our mind stuff. It can also be created during trauma, depression or fear, as it may offer a sensation or illusion of self-control or protection.

The information streaming down meant for us from our Higher-Self will not be able to penetrate the very thick casted man-made metal (a.k.a. patterned thinking, judgment, want, worry or fear-based thinking). The sunlight will not be able to reach us and the body will remain in the darkness with the mind trying to figure out what to do.

When we let our thoughts flow instead of creating this so-called box of armor, we then grant access to our Higher-Self to take the lead.

MOTION

We will now explore how Motion ("to Feel") impacts our lives.

- Flow

- Energy

- Guidance

We are an enigma; mysterious beings attempting to understand this vast universe we live in. In Motion, we have the capacity to initiate an enigmatic place, accessing it when we are creative and using our imagination. When listening to music and swaying to the rhythm, some of us may laugh—taking over all of our senses. It also can be an unexpected tear we have when moved by a profound feeling.

Motion flows throughout the body and leads us to sense the totality of life. It is like a river or a waterfall constantly flowing and circulating back to the ocean. Motion will never try to define our feelings, as it overrides the rational mind. Instead, we trust what we feel and then the Mind can return to what it was always meant to be: the place we access knowledge and relate to the facts and fictions of life.

Motion is like the frequency of a satellite hovering above us, transmitting a signal to a radio. The Mind will acknowledge the music, and by the time we ask what Movement is, we're dancing. Another excellent example is an electric current: it is constantly moving. Electricity is wired to a switch: a device to start and stop the flow of energy. When turned on, the light appears. We acknowledge the electricity because we decided to turn the light on—at no point was the stream of energy turned off.

Water, music and electricity are the perfect examples of one element in the same: the flow of energy.

Motion is completely liberated as it emanates at all times. Everywhere. When we are emotionally and physically relaxed, we have the opportunity to tune into the Motion as it touches our aura; our field of transparent energy surrounding the outer body. Entering Theta brain wave in deep, rested sleep, we access premonition, healing and astral travel. Some of our dreams may offer us insight and guidance as well, especially those we feel really connected to.

Through quieting our Mind to let the thoughts pass and enabling Motion to guide us instead, we can finally transition to a state of a Motion-Mind-Movement Method (to feel, think and act), once again tapping into the primal aspect of our being.

Here, we no longer question life; instead, we attempt to comprehend our life events. The need for psychologically relying on an idea will no longer be necessary because we are focused on our Higher-Self to convey information.

MOVEMENT

Movement ("to Act") is instinctual. It is linked to the subconscious mind of habit, the part of the mind where one is not fully aware, but influences what one does and feels through:

- Action
- Gesture
- Instinct

MIND-MOTION-MOVEMENT METHOD

Movement offers us an option to align with a frequency operating as a superb intelligence moving incredibly fast. Our subconscious actions are based on this, knowing what we need to do, and we simply do it.

Once Movement is mastered, we may discover that Motion prompted us to do or say something to access an Infinite Possibility.

A free thinker must assimilate her own capacity, then decide if she wishes to move forward with an idea or concept. Meaning, she will have self-control and be responsible for her actions. Awareness of our basic mannerisms must be discovered first, as we are habitually creatures of comfort, complacent in a limited place of happily or sadly existing.

---

* Motion

* Movement

* Mind

If we permit Motion to move throughout our body to create a Movement (as opposed to thinking about the Motion), then the Mind will interpret the experience or information without an attachment. It becomes a more natural flow.

I feel - I act - I think is an advanced state of trust and surrender.

I feel, act and think is simultaneously occurring. It is happening.

Now.

It just happened.

Not many are able to accomplish this state; however, the goal may be attained with a commitment of the Motion-Movement-Mind ("MMM") method, and of course, patience.

PATIENCE

Many clients who have completed the Aligning program attempt to incorporate the method in their daily routine and have shared what they go through in the stages of the MMM.

They did understand the concept, but could not always figure out how to apply the process to real life. They claimed they could not interpret the Motion/to Feel and noticed a struggle within their mind when they tried to understand what they were feeling. I suggest we be weary of the addiction most people have to thinking—it will alter the natural flow of Motion. Be sure not to submerge the Self with questions while you're waiting for an answer, like "What does this mean? What is going to happen? Why do I feel this?" If you do, you will lose your sense of clarity and it will bring you back to utilizing the Think/Feel/Act way of being: the Mind-Motion-Movement.

Expectation is basically waiting and delaying one's effort until something else may happen. The body will feel uncomfortable while it has "wants" and waits. Patience is very different than waiting. Our actions show we have confidence and can endure as we trust the process. When we access perseverance as we walk through any given situation, our Higher Intelligence will begin to sense the safety we feel in the body, which requires we recognize what we can and cannot control.

I've learned a simple yet powerful truth: life is an experience we relate to and it is a constant, never-ending transformation. We will have thoughts, feelings and ideas about our experiences. They are only suggestions of a possible actuality we have become co-dependent on.

Please remember to not collapse into any form of instant gratification as you observe your new way of being. You will be challenged by your analytical process during the early stages of your progress, and may find yourself falling back into an old routine of thinking your way through a situation.

Remember you are human. Be easy on yourself. It's okay to have a limited perspective sometimes. The technique will take time. The process may be slow to retrain our body and mind to once again use the Motion-Movement-Mind (Feel-Act-Think) Method instead.

CHAPTER FOURTEEN
HEART CENTER

COMPASS
HEART
MISSION
COMPOSURE
DEVOTION
VULNERABILITY

COMPASS

The Internal Compass resides at the median of the ethereal body at the Heart Center. Like a magnetic compass with a needle mounted on a low-friction pivot point, it can turn easily and smoothly. We use a directional compass to find the direction of north, south, east and west, with a pointer guiding us to "magnetic north." It will spin until it lands on true north.

The Internal Compass is similar, as it points to the Higher-Self. The Higher-Self is our true north, and the magnetic pull is aligning with the Universal Consciousness.

As long as we can find our true north, it will always lead us home. Our Internal Compass can direct all motion and movement in our lives (see *Image 14.1* below).

Image 14.1

INTERNAL COMPASS

HEART

Ahh...the gentle and naïve heart.

I was a young girl romanticizing its meaning with the hopes and wishes of a dreamy true love. Now, just a little bit older, I've cultivated a bit of wisdom regarding the heart and several important aspects. It will pump thousands of gallons of blood throughout the body in a few short days and has its very own electrical current which controls our heart rate.

It is the foundation of our intuition, the very thing that bonds our intuitive and emotional states; a vessel where we are conscious of a right or wrong action. Pursuing matters of the heart, it guides us throughout most of our life's adventures, navigating us to the prime outcome, even when we cannot understand what the end result will be.

It is also the region of the body where we associate and feel Love, one of the most important elements of the human experience.

At its center, we've hidden an imaginary box that holds our dreams, aspirations and our desire to share our secrets. Acceptance is all it knows as it will never judge, allowing the process of giving and receiving.

Interactions founded in Love will influence intimacy. Here we decide to be the most exceptional person offering an open heart to build kindred partnerships based on our feelings.

Even though this is what most people are seeking, we should first value and accept Love for the Self—perhaps creating an optimal relationship with our own hearts, with the intention to understand its language.

Unlike our expressions of affection on the Live Line, authentic love is timeless. This thing called time is an experience measured by our awareness, cognition and action. Honestly, it can only be experienced in the mind and body. Time creates an illusion that Love can be measured by an isolated feeling experienced in the short time we share on an earthbound Live Line.

This is impossible, as Love is eternal!

MISSION

The heart has a frequency that emanates naturally. The Higher-Self ignites this energy, frequency or vibration within us as it gathers in the body at the Heart Center.

Information unknown to us resides within the heart; it is up to you to discover the message. The mind has the tools and will translate the information to register a meaning or association. This is called following the heart, or Motion.

Our lives thrive when we have a mission, although the heart can only feel and cannot define it through words. The act of surrender will aid us in understanding this level of communication and motivate us to walk our own unique path, allowing our mission to be revealed.

COMPOSURE

An individual who has established self-love and worthiness will respond to life's events unlike someone who feels undeserving. There is an unconscious act of respect and compassion for oneself and others. They do not feel privilege, but rather a sense of empowerment because there is an awareness of how they wish to be treated—and it is how they treat others.

When I facilitate an intuitive session with a client who is aligned with her Higher-Self, but not necessarily certain of her life's outcome, her composure in our meeting is to trust the Self and the information presented. The client is aware the experience will empower and offer clarity concerning her life path. I refer to this as surrender: a state where we cease resistance because we feel no opposing action.

There is a huge difference when a client schedules a session with a list of questions and feelings of anxiousness. The client is waiting, hoping and uncertain of her life situation, not trusting the process to unfold on its own.

In the former, there is no co-dependence on the outcome, but rather a natural state of being patient, allowing the process and the mission to be revealed. She has invested in herself, which creates a feeling of self-worth.

DEVOTION

When our actions are founded in authentic love, we give of ourselves without debating if we should or should not. We have no expectation of love or what it will offer us in return. It is not an agreement we make, but perhaps a commitment to remain loyal. There is never a goal when we share our heart with someone.

Devotion is the foundation aligned within our mission. We do because we want to. In fact, most times it's not even a cognitive decision.

Being alive is the glory and privilege to feel, live and love; it is what the body was created to do. We know this because we have felt love and it is lucid, light and free.

VULNERABILITY

Remaining receptive, approachable and without prejudice is required for the heart to stay open and allow all frequencies to flow through. We may lose the freedom to love unconditionally once we have felt hurt, shame or rejection. If we do not release the fear of these experiences, a recurring tendency to protect our vulnerability will arise—a resistance to the free flowing energy of our Heart Center.

This will be evident: we will feel lack, disappointed, frustrated, even curt and short tempered, possibly feeling no motivation to do the things we love. When our heart is blocked, we will feel heavy, disconnected, uninspired, lost or perhaps even depressed. It is important to allow ourselves to be vulnerable; this is how the heart remains open.

We can choose to read books, make promises and create goals, but wanting to discover the heart's mission will not be enough;

it will require much more than any of this. We will need to give
ourselves consent to feel worthy, granting the Self permission to
remain vulnerable and release any unnecessary agreements to
create new commitments. Eventually, we will become devoted to
the heart-centered person we aspire to be.

The Heart Center is where we are aligned to the Higher-Self; we
are navigated there by the Internal Compass. There is no need to
search for true north because our truth lives within us.

CHAPTER FIFTEEN

TRUST

INSTINCT
PSYCHOLOGICAL
PROMISE
BASIC
COURAGE
INTERNAL
INTUITION

INSTINCT

Trust: a deep-rooted comprehension of what is right for you or a twisted knot in your gut knowing what is wrong for you. It is a place we simply surrender into like the sweetest slumber.

We never question the movement of our fingers, arms or legs, as we are reliant on the physiological process.

Trust...is trusting the Self.

It's an unconscious experience we live from moment to moment.

The bridge we walk every day is one step then another, one breath and the next. It is imperative to build on a foundation of trust. It is the primal and necessary element shaping aspects of our entire lives. It requires establishing and supporting loving and authentic relationships with family and friends, as well as with our world structure.

In the next few paragraphs, I will define my theory on trust, based on the concept of the three levels utilized in the Aligning program.

- Psychological Trust
- Basic Trust
- Internal Trust

Each one has its placement within our lives, at various points within our lifetime.

PSYCHOLOGICAL

Psychological Trust: based on your perspective; whatever the outside world promises you in order to move forward with confidence and without fear.

- Thought
- Perception
- Environment

The meaning of true trust has been manipulated. We trust things we see, what people tell us and what they choose to show us. We've accepted the concept that trust is the action we take after some form of acknowledgment has occurred. Our understanding of the situation fulfills the psychological need of what we are told or what we are shown, and thus concludes what we will trust. This level is purely dependent on the perception of our surroundings.

We will take a step if we are shown or told there is solid foundation beneath us; otherwise, we will walk with caution or not move forward at all if we're told the ground is unstable.

Of course this makes sense; knowing we are safe is a natural state of survival. It is why most of us are co-dependent on Psychological Trust. It offers the illusion to help us feel safe in the unpredictable world we live in. This sense of security will allow vulnerability to surface.

We choose to trust when we feel things have settled in our lives, or things are going well, giving us the capacity to move forward with a decision or action.

TRUST

This is not trust, but rather a personal belief. The trust we discuss here is a cognition arising in the mind, deciding on a conclusion which is based on our thoughts, a person or environment.

In relationships, we search for a partner who will present a picture perfect representation to fulfill our needs. In the beginning of a relationship, we will be drawn to a person based on our perception (or what they allow us to see). If our romantic interest does not fit into our expectations, we may become disappointed. For example, he doesn't call as much, or she does not respond to your touch anymore.

We may begin to express a lack of trust within a relationship when we think something is wrong. Believing the person has affected our emotional and mental stability, we conclude and react in a way that does not look like we trust very much. We become suspicious, withdrawn or distracted by something or someone else.

Recognizing when the relationship has changed or ended, we wonder, "What happened to her? Things were so good in the beginning" or "I wish he would be more like he was when we first met."

Resisting change will affect your trust level because things are not altered when we have emotionally invested ourselves; they remain the same...in our mind anyhow. We think life must appear parallel to our beliefs to feel stable. Only then can we roam freely into the world, or at least head into the city to do some shopping.

PROMISE

A promise we make to ourselves could be a first important step in creating positive change, almost like a resolution at the beginning of a new year. However, with some promises made, we intend to never be alone or be emotionally disappointed in a relationship. I'm not sure these are made with integrity; a possible underlying truth to never being alone is to settle with just anyone. Or to not hurt again could imply closing our heart to never love again.

And what is a promise anyhow?

It has nothing to do with reality, but is related to a vow of honor of someone's word, or a suggestion of what you or a person wish to offer. Anyone at any given moment could change their mind, and most likely the change is happening right now. This can be alarming and unsettling to think that what you now know and have based your life on could change in less than a second.

I believe it just changed again.

Psychological trust stuff isn't any fun. In fact, it's a lot of work to invest our energy hoping that things will remain reliable and dependable.

A little story: I knew a few people who believed the Sun revolved around the Earth. When I told them it didn't, there was a lot of resistance and some became angry—until one day they did a little research and found their own proof. You can imagine their devastation as their belief was dismantled.

I use the story of the Sun and Earth because up until several centuries ago, it appeared for so many that the Earth was at the center of our solar system. How powerful to now know the Sun is at its center. This critical information has helped us expand our view of the massive universe we live in, although this knowledge overruled what some believed before.

Most people do not want their concepts questioned or their beliefs rocked.

We must be cautious of the way things appear, especially now in a world focused on social media, which leaves empty spaces in the stories we are told. We should avoid filling in the gaps with what we perceive. What's important for you, the reader, is to be aware of what and how you choose to trust.

BASIC

Basic Trust: a principal right which lives in the body on multiple levels.

- Elemental
- Foundational
- Fundamental

An essential component that most people do not recognize as trust is the primary element of what is most basic in our lives. It is the foundation and starting point of all things. It is so basic it is not even something we acknowledge in our daily routine.

At the end of my day I have a ritual: I wash my face, brush my teeth, put on my PJ's and crawl into my bed. I enter the sacred space called sleep. I position myself to become comfy, tranquil and doze off into a bedtime bliss.

What happens between the closing of my eyes and awakening the next morning is truly unknown to me. I am completely unconscious, though I may remember a dream or two. I do know I went to sleep around 10:30pm, and that my alarm is going off at 5:30am. Never, in all of my life have I ever questioned if I will awaken the next morning. I sleep, I wake up. I know this because I am still here. When I'm sleeping, my heart continues to beat, my blood flows through every organ and my lungs expand as I inhale and exhale.

When we are asleep, the brain and body are doing the physiological work necessary for them to regenerate. Nothing is requested of us, but to simply rest and remember we are taken care of. (Oh good, something less on my to-do list.)

Basic Trust is evident with or without our permission. It is the organic state of the body.

COURAGE

If an individual has experienced trauma, the foundation of Basic Trust may be severed. The threat was so great, the ability to trust was lost and Internal Trust can no longer be grasped. By default, we enter an automatic survival mode dependent on our psychological perspective to have assurance. If Basic Trust is not re-established, we can be challenged by whatever life throws our way.

If this is true for you, or someone you know, some form of healing method will need to transpire. A facilitator can assist in the process of dissolving an impression linked to the trauma. The individual should always use caution, and not attempt to do this on their own, as the issue rises to the surface and may be extremely difficult to process.

The first step to recovery will require acceptance and then release of any mental or emotional attachment to the suffering.

To suffer is always optional.

Courage will be needed, along with a bit of willpower, as the fearless self rises in order for us to prevail. The valor will only be available during the need of a circumstance as we experience difficulty in the present moment.

We cannot step back in time (just yet) and change what has happened. However, we can be brave, kind and gentle to ourselves as we move through our healing process.

INTERNAL

Defining this level of trust may be a bit more challenging than Psychological or Basic. If Psychological Trust is in relation to our environment, then Internal Trust is the complete opposite.

Internal Trust: an instinctual relationship we have with the Self; an internal dialogue based on a clear, healthy emotional and mental state offering us insight and guidance.

- Intuitive
- Intrinsic
- Natural

It will not always be an oral or auditory interaction; it can be a rush of energy or a flash of light. Once we become comfortable with our unique process, we begin to flow naturally in and with our environment. We will never question our insight because it is what we expect for ourselves.

Unless we are in a state of Internal Trust, decision-making will be confusing and require immense effort, leaving us feeling reluctant and unsure. Attempting to approach life events with self-esteem, this is where we appear confident. It is key not to collapse into this fictitious state of self-confidence. Trusting is a whole body experience—a physical, mental and emotional comprehension. It may or may not be personal. Nonetheless, it can be private, hidden or even secret, because sensing an internal connection is an individual's own experience.

INTUITION

Internal Trust is a good gut feeling on a choice you need to make; the dream you had last night that makes no sense, but you know it's important. Or better yet, you're feeling the need to call a friend, then the phone rings and it's her.

It is possible the Universe may offer proof of why you should or shouldn't do something, and I bet most times it will not.

I've learned a valuable lesson from my own experience. I was in the left lane turning on Main Street. I knew I should have not made that turn; however, I was under pressure from the drivers behind me blaring their horns and I decided to go. I did end up in a minor accident. Luckily, no one was injured. I will tell you this: I made an important decision that day. Obviously, most times I will understand how my intuition guides me, and sometimes I will not; nevertheless, I will always trust my gut.

A deep-rooted trust has no need for questions. There is no time for such foolishness because it is acting instinctively, as naturally as you feel at the Heart Center with no hesitation.

The privilege here is you may feel settled and resolved after you've made your decision. You have decided your innermost being will be relieved and celebrated because you have chosen to be reliant on the most important person...you. There will be no fear of being wrong, and especially no need for approval or permission to do what is in your best interest.

Allowing Internal Trust to override Psychological Trust, the mind will no longer be the central decision maker. Alternatively, becoming expectant and comfortable with your intuitive inner dialogue will take precedence.

There are steps you can take to begin to sense your inner dialogue.

Personally, experiencing the awe and beauty of nature, spending time in quiet, being fully present in all things I do and creativity help me resist Psychological Trust. I'll leave you with a bit of inspiration to reflect upon.

- Be still
- Create: draw, color, paint, sew, knit or sculpt
- Sacred space: cultivating a peaceful and calm environment
- Journaling: a resource to release the daily thoughts on paper, instead of making them a permanent place in our head and heart
- Resist multi-tasking
- Relax: be lighthearted, listen to music, sing, dance or play
- Meditation practice

PART IV

FREQUENCY

CHAPTER SIXTEEN
INTERCONNECTED

EXTRAORDINARY
INTELLIGENCE
VEIL
ENERGY
EME

EXTRAORDINARY

You and I are unique, yet the same.

We are having an extraordinary experience in the human body.

Your body and thoughts are shaped differently than mine; however, within us resides the same energy: a frequency, an internal vibration similar to light.

Like me, you may be sensitive in nature. Most likely you have felt this connective energy as it stirs, but haven't quite grasped it on a physical or cognitive level. Even so, we are fully aware it exists as it vibrates in and around us, as well as between all living beings.

I feel privileged to live in an era of transformation where the merging of spirit and science is at the forefront of all we do. Our world is a diverse one where it is no longer necessary to separate our beliefs to represent our fundamental values. There is no need to claim an identity of any sort, a religious belief or a new age lifestyle to feel a sense of connectedness or belonging. Instead, we first must establish a foundation to realign with the Universal Consciousness.

Although some of us will still debate where we fit in, we will need to become tolerant as we witness the breakdown of the barriers that have divided science and the Higher-Self. Science still needs to bridge an Omnipresence at the root of all living things.

Although I'm not sure when, I am certain this discovery will happen. Imagine comprehending this great mystery, the Universal Consciousness and field of frequency.

It will be an extraordinary accomplishment.

INTELLIGENCE

Only a few whom have lived before the twenty-first century have been able to express and document their experience with the Highest Intelligence.

One of the most remarkable beings to walk the Earth in the fifteenth century was Leonardo Da Vinci. A man considered to be a true comprehensive genius, he had accessed a wide range of superpowers, or what we know as intelligence. Some of his areas of interest were mathematics, architecture, science, invention and painting. The *Mona Lisa*, as well as many of his other works of art, is treasured in modern society as a creation of one of the greatest painters of all time.

It would be awesome to meet up with Leonardo and chat over Thai food.

I would carefully plan: wear my best sweater and favorite boots; in my left pocket, I would carry a crystal clear quartz; and I'd bring my journal with a list of questions. I would ask him about his painting technique and drafts of a flying machine, but the most important question I would ask: "Leo, how on Earth did you connect to this heightened intelligence?"

Unfortunately, we were born in different centuries, and I most likely missed the opportunity for one of the most exceptional conversations over pineapple coconut fried rice. So, what is a girl to do, but come to her own conclusion?

See, I believe Leonardo's ample questions and an extensive curiosity allowed him to accept the depth of his mysterious mind; he then applied the rules of logic. I feel somehow he was able to access a higher frequency and was guided by his Higher-Self.

I have no proof as of now; however, I think it's a good theory.

In the next few chapters, we will cover this very topic of an enhanced intelligence. The approach is unique and based on the Aligning Method. The knowledge is not necessary, but it will be needed to access the creative process within the field of Infinite Perception.

I suggest you take your time reading and re-reading this again, as it is an advanced concept I am sharing, perhaps expressed in a new way. Please know it is not necessary to relate to the formula, but rather to create a simple comprehension of the way we utilize this frequency and how we may reconnect to it.

VEIL

There are realms unknown to us beyond this space and time: transparent portals which reach the ends of our universe and bridge into others; a gateway into the Unknown exists there. A thin veil which lies between this moment and the next.

The past, future, spirit, celestial realms, our guides and the Higher-Self reside here as well. At times we may be able to navigate through this translucent fabric. If we have a clear mind and an open heart, our senses may initiate access to what is beyond the veil.

ENERGY

The sun, moon, sky, you and the universe: everything is energy.

Imagine a spool of thread endlessly unraveling, moving like a wave having the ability to wander where it wants, here and there, surrounding you, me and everyone at this exact moment. It has the capacity to transverse like turning on a light or a radio filling the room. We can see the visible light. We can feel the vibration of the radio waves emanating from a song.

Sunlight streams through the transparent glass walls of a skyscraper, reaching the first and the 90th floor of a building at the same time. The moon shines, illuminating our city and brightly seeping in through our bedroom window.

We experience energy all the time within an electromagnetic spectrum, which consists of radio waves, microwaves, infrared radiation, visible light, ultraviolet radiation, X-ray and gamma rays. It is the elemental foundation of the world we live in.

One of the most vital elements for the Earth is the Sun. Its light is energy and illuminates our world.

We feel and see the Sun's light rays, which is equal to electromagnetic energy. It radiates visible light our eyes can detect. When conveyed, a frequency is expressed, and then our eyes take in the colors, shapes and dimension of our experience here on Earth.

The spectrum also contains information our vision and our brain cannot recognize, as the human eye cannot respond to the higher frequency and shorter wavelength of the spectrum.

Ultraviolet is a higher frequency with a shorter wavelength, and an important component of sunlight for the production of Vitamin D. The ozone layer blocks most of it so as not to touch the Earth's surface, as too much exposure can be harmful and lead to sunburn, or even worse: skin cancer. (I highly suggest you wear your sunscreen people!)

The point I'm attempting to make: ultraviolet rays cannot be seen, but they still stream down to the Earth and are absorbed by the body.

EME

The Sun's ray of energy allows us to only have a partial visual experience in our daily lives. Electromagnetic Energy (EME) offers 100% of an unseen amount of information and substance we cannot perceive. It is like having a partial view of a road or a village; basically, a limited perception of our world and the multi-dimensional Universe. A living system of life we cannot see; nonetheless, it still exists.

Yes, just the thought can be overwhelming, so let's use this example to define it more clearly. I'll use one of my favorite places to tell our story.

I am at the beach.

I am sitting here enjoying a Granny Smith apple.

You cannot see me.

You are there, reading this sentence, perhaps on the same beach.

I cannot see you.

Nonetheless, you are there and I am here.

The same applies for a surfer on a beach in Australia, making his way to the most amazing wave.

You are reading this sentence.

I'm here.

The Australian is there.

We all exist.

The Australian does exist, just as much as you and I, though we cannot see each other and do not concern ourselves with the debate if we exist or not. We are completely unconscious of each other's actions or appearance. To stereotype the surfer, my mind immediately assumes he is tall (let's make him 6'4), with a strong build and most likely beach blonde. No proof for this one; he might as well be 5'6 and dark-haired.

EME is a frequency or wave of energy traveling at 100 percent. It has the ability to oscillate through the veil I mentioned earlier, with different levels of energy moving at the same time around and around, clockwise and counter-clockwise, up and down within itself...I hope you are getting the picture.

You are here.

I'm here.

The Australian is here.

We all exist.

We are all here.

In the present.

EME is expressing what our simple sight cannot comprehend, just like X-rays or gamma waves.

Offering us the relationship with an abundant amount of frequencies, we have possibilities or opportunities. We have the option to sense and interact with an Infinite Possibility as we live life simultaneously. I did say sense and not see. We must remember the human eyes are limited to what is right here in front of us. The mind cannot understand something that has yet to be experienced; it does not comprehend the Unknown.

Having an experience with energy at one hundred percent:

I am sitting here writing.

I am able to sense you reading this sentence.

I am able to acknowledge the Australian surfer (dark hair).

I am able to hear the planet Neptune spin very slowly.

I can feel celestial beings and guides.

A spirit of a deceased family member waves hello.

I can see aliens time-traveling through the eighth dimension.

I recognize the past and change an event that has touched my life in some way.

I am aware of future opportunities unfolding and choose the very best one.

Although this sounds awesome and impossible to believe, what's important is that we are attentive to the perspective of the Higher-Self as it observes the lower-self on the Live Line in the present moment.

Through our capacity to access information from the Higher-Self's perspective, we begin to ride the wave of frequency in the field of Electromagnetic Energy. The opportunity will appear for us to salute the cute Australian surfing, and we also experience the unlimited options and the threads that link us.

CHAPTER SEVENTEEN

THREADS

HARMONY
ACCEPTANCE
DESTINED

"An invisible thread connects those destined to meet, regardless of time, place and circumstance. The thread will expand, stretch or tangle; however, it will never break." Ancient Chinese Proverb

---

HARMONY

The Higher-Self and lower-self have a complex foundation of alignment and harmony, interacting between all levels of time and space. In the theory of the Aligning Method, the Threads exist on an ethereal level acting like electricity. It is similar to an interlaced ball of yarn spinning with infinite layers crossing left/right, up/down, inward/outward, interlocked within all living beings. It can never be broken, severed or disconnected.

Sensing the animation of the Threads in motion would be equivalent to musical notes written for musicians. When read, the instruments channel all the elements brought together to create a harmony. Visualize a pen and its ink creating letters, and then we have words on paper.

Although this action of the ink and writing appear separated, or in stages, the pen created one word and then another supporting the next, even if the sentences are on different pages. A word on page one has not yet discovered the word on page 39. This does not matter as they support the whole story; because in the process of the author writing, they become one.

The same holds true for the series of novels I've been attempting to read forever. The author's perspective of writing a novel series: the first book is written in its entirety and can stand alone, but when the second book is written, it is rippling into the next. The characters interact as the author writes; however, he may not always be aware of how they will become weaved within the storyline.

Imagine reading the second book in the series of three before the first. We would become a bit confused, as we would not understand the premise of the storyline. Yet, when we begin to read the first book, it would almost be like time-traveling to the beginning of the story. We begin to discover the stages of the characters and their relationship as they developed in the past, and then we read the most recent novel to become aware of what will happen next.

ACCEPTANCE

Our relation to the Threads link us to the ones we love, a stranger or the ones that disappoint us on our life path. We will not always understand the meaning of the multi-layered events the Threads inspire. At times they will become tangled; this is not positive or negative. It is energy playing out its role to assist us.

It is intertwined with the possible resolution where we can recognize the precise correlation; what has caused you to feel the entanglement; and an insight to resolve it.

First, we must approach the situation without judgment. We may be able to alter our focus to acceptance. We are aware the link can never be severed; however, once completed or satisfied, we may be able to let go of a mental or emotional charge related to the event. In doing so, we establish a non-attached mindset of the matter to find clarity, feeling liberated from a situation so a possible Symmetry may occur.

DESTINED

Accepting that there is a purpose of the Threads can help us to comprehend the possible meaning of a situation; perhaps allowing us to find peace. It opens the door to an unconscious shift, one in which we remove blocked and inauthentic energy.

Acceptance will remove any resistance, allowing the universal signs and symbols to be revealed. From here, we may be able to start working on the release of what is known as "Karma." In Buddhism and Hinduism, Karma is viewed as deciding a fate in future existences. I have my own take on Karma: our authentic actions in life and previous states of existence will serve our true cause.

It is actually fortunate when we stumble upon one of the many soulmates we are destined to meet as part of our Karma; they may hold the key to unraveling the subconscious experiences we hold within our being. In accepting these destined threads without attachment, we are given the opportunity to learn more about ourselves and humankind.

CHAPTER EIGHTEEN

SYMMETRY

REFLECTION
INFLUENCE
AWARENESS

REFLECTION

We will mirror each other standing face to face, and at other times leaning back to back. A reflection in more ways than one, resembling one another without being identical; perhaps, a likeness, but still unique in our own way, becoming conscious of the other's presence when our frequency has realigned.

Symmetry sets the stage for an intricate design of art, architecture and music and can be found in physics and nature. Appearing in many forms in our world, I also recognize it as the foundation within the frequency of one's life path. In this aspect, it can be:

- A harmony of absolute coherent perfection within order or chaos
- Precisely comparable energies reflecting each other
- Similar correspondence between a contrasting structure or form

Symmetry is supporting the energy running through the center of all things; the Threads we have become familiar with.

Each and every one of us has our own unique life path. Our surroundings may assist in a potential understanding of an action required to live authentically. Therefore, we may shift when our frequency aligns with an experience or another human being.

We may feel elated. This is Symmetry.

We may also feel miserable. This is Symmetry.

Life's events call on us or attract us, and we gravitate toward one or another. Our perception of the person or situation will make us feel comfortable or uneasy. This is Symmetry attempting to make us conscious of the responsibility to live in accordance with our highest good. It may also be alerting us of an opportunity to work out an entanglement, which may belong to you or the person(s) involved.

Symmetry is integrated into one's life by acting out its intent. We need to remain factual as we move through the situation, and it can only be approached with compassion and fairness to evolve. If we do not complete the Symmetry, no worries—it will come back around, perhaps next month, in a century or on another elemental plane.

Be careful with this one; there will be many contributing factors and we may not always have the choice to confront our Symmetry as we see suitable.

Note: At no point does Symmetry mean the individual should remain in a situation that causes harm or suffering to oneself or another.

INFLUENCE

I recall packing for my travels to Sedona. I had a strong desire to create a coalition to serve "my" battle to create a safe space for our children.

SYMMETRY

A realization brought awareness to how my childhood experience contributed to my choices. I became conscious of what was at the foundation of my own Symmetry.

I've found much clarity as I refused to continue the cycle founded in fear, feeling liberated to no longer act out of a painful childhood story of a little girl in need of protection. Today, I choose to purely teach children The Eight Second Rule to remain peaceful, and am no longer motivated by an unconscious act to fix my own childhood memories of pain and suffering.

I have established that Threads and Symmetry exist on and within, as well as across, an infinite multidimensional level. Their interaction within our existence will evolve at the immeasurable beginning and end of time. Their frequency is oscillating internally and externally, instantaneously sending out a current aligned with our life purpose.

Our intention must be fulfilled; the influence will be so strong it will override any conscious thought or action. We may not always understand the motivation behind our actions, but we will be drawn in and to it.

I feel it is important we mention the Golden Rule when discussing this theory.

The Golden Rule: a defined behavior where an individual would like to be treated as he treats others. The Golden Rule is an approach many have taken and assumed as a moral act based on one's integrity. It makes common sense as a human courtesy.

The Golden Rule applies to our principles established in policies, rules or beliefs, which have no foundation or relevance within the Threads. We are aligning with an elaborate plan, and the unrestricted laws of a universal energy. Our personal opinions do not reside there; only a high and a low frequency.

High frequency: we align with the Higher-Self, which is living in our integrity, an authenticity linked to what is true. When we feel joy, we experience it and let it go. If we feel anger, we experience it and then we let it go. We cannot hold onto the emotion for long, as we lose the opportunity for the next authentic feeling.

Lower frequency: an experience we only have on the Live Line based on our beliefs or concepts. For example, we tend to hold onto happiness or sadness when we feel it. We think we will lose the feeling of happiness and never have it again, or if we let go of this sadness, we will experience a feeling of something much worse.

AWARENESS

Equilibrium of our own frequency must first occur for a change to materialize here on the Live Line; meaning, we must first create physical, mental and emotional stability. Ultimately, we have the power to create balance as our consciousness awakens.

Interacting among family, friends or even a stranger, our foundation must remain neutral and grounded; we must refrain from leaving our center. We do our best not to take on another's actions, knowing this has nothing to with us on a personal level. It is our awareness that helps us remain stable within the interaction.

I would like to propose a compassionate social interaction with our community that will send a message to see humankind as oneself. We have a responsibility to utilize this awareness as we arc not ignorant to the key we hold to create change. It is only a being with a human consciousness that has the power to choose for oneself, with the hope that a potential Symmetry will be used as a gateway to self-realization.

A THEORY: QUANTUM ENTANGLEMENT

I'm fascinated by science and physics; however, I'm simply a novice with the desire to learn. I'm hoping a short description will help further define the meaning of frequency founded in the Aligning Method.

There is a theory in physics called quantum entanglement, and I believe it supports the idea of Symmetry.

Imagine we have a ball of clay sitting here in Long Island, New York. We split the clay and it propels itself 100 light years across the universe. The clay here in New York begins to spin clockwise; based on the theory in quantum physics, the piece of clay 100 light years away will also begin to turn. They are unified always! The split or separation does not apply on an energy level.

My conclusion: Quantum Entanglement is deeply rooted in the foundation of the Threads and Symmetry.

CHAPTER NINETEEN

INFINITE

IMMEASURABLE
LOVE
POSSIBILITIES
LIMITLESS
INNOVATOR
MANIFEST

INFINITE (ˈin-fə-nət)

1. extending indefinitely; endless infinite space.

2. immeasurably or inconceivably great or extensive; inexhaustible.

3. subject to no limitation or external determination.

4. a. extending beyond, lying beyond or being greater than any preassigned value however large.
    b. extending to infinity.
    c. characterized by an infinite number of elements or terms.

Credit: Merriam Webster Dictionary

IMMEASURABLE

I wonder how deep the ocean is.

I contemplate our endless expanding universe.

I imagine the meaning of Infinite and I feel the immeasurable love I have for my daughter.

It is intense and offers a sense of comfort, acceptance and completely giving of myself wholeheartedly.

As a mother, I will do whatever it takes to provide an environment where she may blossom into a healthy young woman. I have chosen to create a safe space and I call it home. I know I will carry out this responsibility forevermore.

I cannot even fathom this love I feel for my girl; it will never fade. I know when she is attending college or has a family of her own,

I will still feel her love. I know my love will not end when it is my time to leave this Earth plane. Although, I presume it will intensify and expand in some way, and I look forward to the days it will.

This intense emotion I have for my daughter reminds me we are Infinite.

Infinite appears never-ending.

It has been, will be, always:

- Eternal
- Expansive
- Constant

If I attempt to understand the true definition, I know I cannot grasp its significance because I am utilizing my mind's focus solely on what is finite; a restricted view of my life on the linear line.

We are given an opportunity to comprehend something of great importance. We are:

- Limitless
- Boundless
- Timeless

It does not begin here.

It does not end here.

Yes, I believe we extend beyond our conscious thought and mind. It is possible we came from somewhere to learn, live and love for just a little while. I have a good gut feeling some part of us, perhaps our essence, continues on.

LOVE

I think I've done a pretty good job to solidify the meaning of Infinite as eternal. Well, then we will need to establish Love with a similar definition.

But first, we will need to remove any confusion we may feel about this emotionally driven energy that is restricted to the complex association of relationships. It is so much more than the limitations of our human interaction. Sadly, we may believe it is similar to an experience on the Live Line, limited to a start and finish, beginning and end or even a birth and death.

This cannot be so, as the glorious meaning of Love is instilled at the core of our being. Opening our hearts to the beauty of life offers us a comprehension of absolute unity, existing as a magnificent frequency within the depth of our psyche. It has no goal, and I promise you it will override any predetermined plan we may create.

Love cannot be measured, compromised or affected by an outside influence. It will never be defeated and knows no threat of shame, loss or even death.

Aligning Infinite and Love, we ignite a gateway to boundless potential, wholeness and interconnectedness. Literally, it will kindle the discovery of our like-minded tribe to touch our soul. We will be supported; to never walk alone or need a resolution to our Karma.

If we lose something so precious as life and Love, we believe it is gone forever, evoking a human condition of sorrow. It makes sense, and I understand this all too well. However, we should not fall victim to our cognitive approach by creating the illusion that Love will end within the limited timeframe we have in our relationships.

Love does not randomly appear or disappear; it is always right here. We simply awaken to its presence, or perchance, we stumble upon it.

Love can never die. It is pure, wild and free.

I've watched those close to me attempt to contain, control or even tame this uncharted energy, and they were not successful. Honestly, choosing to do so would be to close oneself off to being loved to protect our vulnerability and insecurities.

The individual must remain open as Love carries the essential elements of our existence. Infinite Love can never be received, given or lost. I'm sure it will not care if we choose to acknowledge or deny its presence.

Infinitely existing before we were born, it will remain after the body dies.

POSSIBILITIES

I think we should meet.

Yes, you and I will randomly have an encounter somewhere. Let's choose the fresh crisp mountain air of Boulder, Colorado.

INFINITE

We will meet across Pearl Street, at a warm, quiet bookstore
fragrant with freshly bound books and bold roasted coffee, two
cups with coconut creamer in hand. We stumble upon two plum
colored cozy armchairs. You sit first. I follow and sit right across
from you with a backdrop of shelves as high as the ceiling,
holding thousands of books. Sitting, we fall quietly yet deeply into
a conversation about Infinite Possibilities.

To save us from cold coffee, I will attempt to breakdown the
concept.

Infinite Possibilities: abundant unlimited opportunity and
boundless never-ending options, founded within a state of:

- Unconditional
- Intuitive
- Randomness

Let's detail.

The last second; yes, the one before this one has created this
experience based on your thought, emotion and frequency.

In one day, we will experience 86,400 seconds. One possible
moment in your life is unconditional and intuitively chosen at
random. Our life on the Live Line offers unlimited opportunity for
an Infinite Possibility, which means we have the power to create
anything no less than amazing.

Imagine you have endless photo albums filled with an infinite
amount of Polaroids. Each page in your photo book represents

193

a second. On each page, we have 100 Polaroids representing an option. Each Polaroid is a link to the possible next second.

The photo you choose leads to another page with the next 100 Polaroids. The photo you choose there leads to the following page...and so on. The album represents our life as a whole and the photos are linked to the infinite amount of possible scenarios. Consciously or unconsciously, we choose to create our experiences moment by moment.

Now, imagine opening a new photo album leading to an entirely different path for oneself; an Infinite Possibility yet uncovered. It would be like taking a quantum leap, accelerating from one moment to the next. Not in a hurried or hasty jump, but a gentle soar dependent on our intuitive selection.

LIMITLESS

And now, I'll wait for all the "What do you mean here?" questions and moans after you read this paragraph.

Light speed moves just under 200,000 miles per second. Imagine taking a super fast trip around the world. If we could travel at the speed of light, it would be a short one circling the Earth at just about 7.5 times in one second. (The mind's mental observation would find this impossible to watch, no less comprehend, the movement).

It is said no single thing has the ability to travel faster than light. However, I have a theory: perhaps light travels so fast it appears to stand still and does not move at all. Similar to the Polaroid laying still in your photo album waiting to be chosen.

Perhaps each Polaroid represents a light speed second, with one photo supporting the one before and the one after. Ultimately, each offers the option, when combined, to create an extraordinary slide show of our lives.

This is a lot to take in, and I can imagine a challenge to process. It's amusing—after all of these years defining the theory, I still get a little brain fog thinking of the concept.

The incredible unfolding of being guided by the Higher-Self sets things in motion, and somehow they show up. Events play out with perfection when we're *Living Aligned*.

I'm smiling while my coffee is still warm and the Boulder Book shop is just near closing. You can debate my cozy book store story. Regardless of whether you believe it or not, we have limitless potential. Consciously, we simply need to remain at our center, trust and surrender to the process to access an Infinite Possibility.

INNOVATOR

Innovation is a random act of the most optimal opportunity carefully calculated for the Live Line. The event can only be created and acknowledged by the Higher-Self. At times, we will observe a magical unfolding of the Threads interlocking in relation to our Symmetry.

Ultimately, we have only one Infinite limitless option at a time, which will lead to the next best Infinite chance. The Higher-Self retrieves a unique possibility to create our reality. Our authentic story has been written and placed upon a never-ending bookshelf somewhere. When we are living in our integrity and authenticity, a Symmetry occurs. Here we have the ability to access a light speed moment to choose an optimal page in a chapter we would like to create on the Live Line.

MANIFEST

Several years ago, a few friends were rushing to the local Barnes and Noble to purchase books on manifestation and the laws of attraction process (be positive, think about what you would like and poof, it appears).

I was curious to know more about the approach, so I recall picking up a book a girlfriend had suggested. After reading it from cover to cover, I felt a bit confused because there were a few statements on being positive and a vague description on the steps.

Eventually, I saw no true tools on how to attract a soulmate, become a zillionaire or save the planet. If there were such a formula, it appeared it was missing, or maybe the authors were keeping it for themselves. All humor aside, I've come to believe we need no instructions, manuals or directions. Although it is required we summon our brilliance, remember we have the ability to create our own magnificence.

This happens naturally when we are *Living Aligned*. All we need to do is tap into the great field of energy that holds what is meant for us; an internal gateway to abundance. Our life path waits patiently for a sign that we are grounded and ready to welcome an experience of perfection.

We become the inventor of the invention; we are not what is invented, but the vessel that allows it to pour through and present itself.

Embracing the title as the innovator, our ability will resurface to transform one amazing path into reality. Think of how the great innovators, such as Tesla, Da Vinci and Einstein, were inspired and motivated by an intention greater than their own.

Our commitment to dream up something spectacular must be formulated within an Infinite Possibility. If we utilize wishful thinking, we will not align with what is unconditional on the energy plane, and therefore, cannot invent it here on the Live Line. We can design an experience, perhaps replicating similar patterns of our past or inviting something that looks like what we wanted. In spite of our efforts, it will not be the real thing.

Please take into account your responsibility of being neutral and non-attached before you decide to take on the title of the innovator.

Imagine holding in your hands the photo album of your soul's journey. Turning page after page of all the events of your life's adventure, and you will find them perfectly lined up as they should be. I think we'd be surprised to discover how truly simple it would be to access our true life path filled with beauty, bravery and Bliss.

CHAPTER TWENTY

BLISS

GRATITUDE
IGNORANCE
ENCHANTED
UNCONDITIONAL
CHOICE

GRATITUDE

We all wish to be held, and in some way regarded, honored or respected; simply loved. I believe it is because Love offers us a promise that we will always be safe, taken care of and provided for, and helps us to recognize we are deserving and worthy.

It creates a mental and emotional state of complete gratitude for all that we are and have.

My search for this love was put to an end many summers ago in Sedona, when I decided I would no longer be consumed with the thought of finding love with another. My decision made room for a sense of wonder out West. I tapped into a profound feeling and called it Bliss. I became crystal clear and ready to receive. As I said "Apple" and named it "Blue," I had made a request and then it was given. We know how the story unfolds from the first chapter.

Upon my return to the East Coast, I began to contemplate this notion of Bliss and the euphoric feeling that came with it. Realizing we have all we need and that we are unified with the Universal Consciousness was quite liberating. The sensation was enchanting, though a bit much to digest, as I still cannot define it with words. My thoughts persisted about how could I hold on to this feeling: when one is elated, how it can be exposed, shared and integrated into everyday life.

I believed it was the key to peace, healing, abundance, innovation…everything.

The question urged me to explore what it really meant and to describe its absolute meaning.

IGNORANCE

There is a statement I've heard since childhood among my family and friends. In a distant and small circle of my father's friends, I would hear comments made when someone was lighthearted, innocent, silly, clumsy or not aware of the truth. Always smiling as they whispered under their breaths, "Ignorance is Bliss." It was based on their judgment and holds no weight on my own opinion. Nevertheless, we will use it as a way to define.

It is said that ignorance is Bliss; however, I do not agree. They may appear similar, but are not the same.

Bliss is like a doubled-sided coin, where each side is carefree and presents a sense of innocence. Although the ignorant side of the coin sees life happily, it has a limited perception, a lack of knowledge and lives unconsciously. It possibly conducts itself as untouchable and may be defensive of its concepts and beliefs.

The blissful side of the coin is invincible and has gratitude for all of its experiences, may they be positive or negative. Random feelings of enchantment, exhilaration and delight are invigorating as options and opportunities are revealed.

Bliss has a complete awareness of all life's hardships, yet it will choose to remain in gratitude and stay grounded, established within its truth and without an attachment to struggle, suffering or tragedy.

ENCHANTED

I truly believe we once lived in a magical state as old as our souls; an innocence of limitless potential of the imagination, a place only accessed when we are children, being peaceful, playful or creative.

I suppose it did not hold such importance in our youth, as it was left behind when it was time to grow up. We needed to prepare for the real world, and joining a civilized society became our priority. Our parents, caregivers and teachers believed they were offering support by gently coercing us to decide that the tangible responsibilities of education, bills and relationships were more important than living enchanted.

Sooner than later, we were subjected to creating a master plan of ideal concepts we hoped would offer us success and satisfaction, or perhaps a fortress of protection from the fearful possibilities of heartbreak, loneliness or not having enough.

We should observe and learn from our children in their routine as they entertain themselves simply to live unconditionally; create, laugh, cry, play and create once more. A child is not defensive or protective because she feels no threat of being vulnerable. She is unconsciously aware of the need to surrender to her imagination, the place where she comprehends all things are possible. Being enchanted is her natural state; it is who she is, and will intend to remain as she grows older.

Bliss makes a promise that enchantment can happen at any given moment.

Bliss is more than a happy, emotionally-defined belief system that can be explained. It is pure, euphoric and leads to rapture which cannot be conformed. It extends and expands itself outside the body, where the brink between an Omnipresence and the Earth plane reside, illuminating a vast space precisely, infinitely lucid without ambivalence.

The realization, "You Have All You Need" is linked to what is above and beyond the Live Line. If we acknowledge and practice with a foundation of Bliss, we may activate the magnetic field within the Heart Center. The Internal Compass will once again align with the multi-dimensional energy of the Threads and Symmetry that we as mortals and a Universal Consciousness co-exist within.

UNCONDITIONAL

I hope I have at least captured the essence of this celestial feeling with mere words. I battled for months with a rational mind attempting to grasp the meaning, yet still no words held an accurate understanding to convey its true expression. Although friends and clients still asked if I could define the feeling, I suppose I would choose the words innocence and enchanted.

However, unconditional would be the one that holds most true, ultimately meaning to be without restriction. A profound sensory within the Self, pure without thought or motivation. A united transparency integrated with a fundamental value of compassion and integrity.

I have seen, felt and heard of many miracles in this extraordinarily life. I suppose you have as well. I imagine at one point we all will experience wonder or a phenomenon we cannot explain, and we may not have the need or comprehension to.

CHOICE

This manuscript opened the conversation to the profound epiphany I've experienced. The theory is a solid interpretation of a unified structure of frequency we all have access to. I feel it is this very field that offers the opportunity to discover our Higher Intelligence.

The words and thoughts expressed in the chapters reflect my personal journey. I understand that to relate or apply the Method could be challenging in the beginning. All I ask of you is to be open to make the choice to approach life with love, honor and embrace the present moment. Acknowledge we are provided for and have all we need within us.

The Higher-Self wants us to remember:

- Be here, in the present moment
- Breathe
- Realign with the vital life force
- Remain centered

- Detachment and non-judgment will help us remain clear
- Suffering is not an option
- All things are temporary
- Observe what you think, feel and create
- Access the Internal Compass at your Heart Center
- Surrender to comprehend the true meaning of Trust
- Be compassionate
- Live authentically
- Remain within your integrity
- Recognize your courage
- Be aware of your Symmetry
- Higher-Self always guides us
- We have access to Infinite Possibilities
- We are Unconditional
- We are interlocked with an Omnipresence
- You are the Innovator
- Bliss is our natural state

Ultimately, we have a choice to smile at one another. Be kind. Be patient. Be compassionate. Be Love. Live life in gratitude. Comprehend we are linked to something grand: unconditional Love and peace.

CONCLUSION

CONCLUSION

While revisiting a few of the chapters, I realized there was
so much more I wanted to share. I will not be able to cover
everything in the conclusion as there is an abundant amount of
information. However, to simplify, I will add a few insights.

Several years ago, *Living Aligned* started out as a manual. In the
beginning stages of the rough draft, it dawned on me that no one
really wants to be told what to do. Rather, we are seeking out that
one inspired moment to shift our perception with the promise
it will change us forever. Luckily, before I deleted the first file, I
took from it what I felt would benefit the reader and started fresh.

The *Living Aligned* manuscript was not intended to be about the
spiritual and personal development within the Aligning program,
but my attempt to explain the concept as it could aid someone's
healing and enlightenment. My intention is for the individual
reading to understand what we can accomplish if we are
committed to living in peace, integrity and unconditional love.

A little light turned on somewhere in my head and heart when I
decided to share some of my stories as part of the foundation of
the Aligning Method. I hope and trust in some way the book has
inspired your own light to be shared or perhaps illuminated the
path to discover your own blissful state.

My practice of the Aligning Method required that I make many
changes in my own life, one being that I still use the Eight Second
Rule. Yes, I inhale, exhale, then decide if I wish to engage with a
thought or situation.

Another being a really powerful decision: I no longer live with
conflict or uncertainty.

I truly have created a harmony and foundation of unconditional authenticity. For me, this has led to a peaceful and liberated life. What occurred so many years ago out West truly altered my existence. It was crystal clear what Sedona needed of me, and sharing the comprehension of this link we have with Universal Consciousness and the Higher-Self was extremely important. The commitment to write has remained throughout an all-encompassing heartfelt five years.

Today, I am still unfolding into the process as I am facilitating the program and am at the beginning stages of certifying others who have potential to teach the Aligning Method as well.

The purpose is to always assist individuals to realign with their Higher-Self, to access intuition and if needed, to heal their heart and mind.

To guide them to return to their natural state of alignment and remember...we have all we need.

Peace and bliss to you and yours,

Kathrine

GLOSSARY

Ananda: extreme happiness, feeling blessed, highest states of being. (Sanskrit: rooted in Eastern philosophies of Hinduism, Buddhism and Jainism)

Astrology: study of the planetary and celestial movements having an influence on human affairs and the natural world

Authenticity: true, real

Bliss: euphoria, elation

Chakra: Yoga/Hindu philosophy, Sanskrit; energy centers in the human body

Center: peace, grounded, neutral

Ethereal: non-material, intangible, transcendent, otherworldly

Eight Second Rule: breathing exercise to calm and center the mind and body

Eight Limbs Path: Sanskrit term, Ashtanga, referring to aspects of the yogic path

EME: electromagnetic field of energy

Feng Shui: system governed on placement and flow of energy

Frequency: energy, vibration, constituting a wave, in a material (as in sound waves) or in an electromagnetic field (as in radio waves and light), usually measured per second

Golden Rule: basic principle rule of morality, ethics

Higher-Self: essence, soul, Higher Intelligence

Innovator: inventor, conduit

Intuition: instinctive feeling, insight

Integer: whole number, not a fraction, complete in itself

Live Line: Earth, past-present-future

Impression: auditory, visual, olfactory linked to subconscious

Perception: sensory without limitation

Infinite Possibility: limitless opportunity

Mantra: word, sound repeated to aid in meditation practice

Mind: to think, access knowledge, beliefs, concepts

Mindfulness: mental state achieved by focusing one's awareness on the present moment

Motion: to feel, fluid energy, intuition

Movement: to act, decision

Neutral: impartial, detached, centered

Omnipresent: universal consciousness, all places simultaneously, constant

Right-Action: decision based on gut feeling, intuition

GLOSSARY

Reiki: healing technique to restore physical and emotional well-being

Savasana: resting, or corpse pose in Hatha yoga

Selective Amnesia: a fragmented memory

Symmetry: aligned frequency/energy, similar

Subconscious: part of the mind one is not fully aware of, but influences one's actions and feelings

Tao Te Ching: 81 verses inspired by Zen philosophy, Lao Tzu

Threads: current, connection, interlocking

Transcendent: beyond physical human experience

Trust: certainty, to decide without hesitation

Universal Consciousness: Omnipresence, unified

Vertex: crown, highest point

Yoga: union, Hindu practice of meditation, posture, actions

Zen: to achieve enlightenment and intuition through meditation to transcend rational thought and action

ABOUT THE AUTHOR

Kathrine Mitchell, Intuitive, Author, Transformational Life Coach and Teacher of Yoga and Meditation, is the founder of the Aligning program. Spanning over three decades of service, her intention is to innovatively share insight and help others discover their own unique journey. Her lifelong mission has been to empower individuals to experience strength, peace and enlightenment—the foundation for *Living Aligned*.

Also an artist by nature, Kathrine founded Rooted In The Earth™, featuring a collection of sacred stones and symbols aligned with precious metals. She lives with her daughter along the South Shore of Long Island, New York, where she finds her personal inspiration and bliss by the ocean.

To contact Kathrine, you can email her at kat@kathrinemitchell.com or visit her website at www.kathrinemitchell.com.

INTERNAL COMPASS

While *Living Aligned* will inspire us to reconnect to our Higher-Self, Kathrine's forthcoming manuscript, *Internal Compass,* will ignite the Heart Center so we may learn to trust, live with certainty, access our intuitive intelligence and find our true north.

CREDITS

Special thanks to my publishing team:
Editor: Jennifer Dee
Cover Art: Steven Gagliano
Photographer: Janel Lombardi
Hair/Makeup: Christina Aprile
Published by Aligning Inc. 2020

www.ingramcontent.com/pod-product-compliance
Lightning Source LLC
Chambersburg PA
CBHW060644150426
42811CB00079B/2313/J

NAOMI FINDLAY

SELL YOUR PROPERTY FOR MORE MONEY

Naomi Findlay PhD
BEST SELLING AUTHOR

contents